CW01663463

Val Stones

The cake whisperer!

Bake with
Love
Val

London

Val Stones

The cake whisperer!

52 recipes to
make with love

archetype books

First published in Great Britain in 2018
by Archetype Books.

A CIP record of this book is available from the British Library.

ISBN 978 1 9997637 2 5

Design: Michael Phillips

Editing: Marianne Ryan

Photography: Val Stones

Front cover photograph: Katharine Davies

Additional photography: Katharine Davies, Selasi Gbormittah, Love Productions, Andrew Melville, Denise Melville, Hannah Pereira, Michael Phillips

Printed in China

Sponsors: Harts of Stur for enabling the index, Vivienne Clore for funding early copies, and Billington's Sugar for providing sugars and flour for recipe development

Archetype Books
Clarendon House
52 Cornmarket Street
Oxford, OX1 3HJ
United Kingdom

archetypebooks.net

Dedicated to my grandchildren Arthur and William

Contents

My daughter and son, Elizabeth and Richard

My mother and me!

My grandchildren, William (left) and Arthur

Introduction

'Anyone can be a good cook, the secret to success is chiefly attention to detail – partly an adventurous spirit.'

Woman's Home Cook Book 1964

The above quote is from one of my very first cook books; I was fourteen and just setting out on the adventure of learning to bake – the passion came later. When folk ask me 'who taught you to bake?' I say, 'One Mum, one mum-in- law, four grandmas and five aunties'. I must not forget the others, the Be-Ro book, Mary Berry, Marguerite Patten, Prue Leith, Delia Smith, Dan Lepard and Michel Roux.

Life has a funny way of surprising you when you least expect it. I always tell folk that I have been lucky enough to have led a gifted life. I have had a teaching career that I loved and along the way my passion for baking has brought me interest and relaxation.

But when you think you have given all you can and it's time to retire, what did I do? In 2016 I applied to go on The Great British Bake Off and was accepted. On the programme, I was known for exercising while I baked, but also for listening to my cakes to hear when they were ready – I call myself 'The Cake Whisperer'!

What many people don't know is that I was a primary teacher for forty years and a head teacher for thirteen years.

Another thing that people don't know is that I am dyslexic and aged eleven I wasn't a fluent reader. I knew I wasn't stupid because I had a photographic memory but sadly dyslexia wasn't known as such then and I wasn't given the learning opportunities that would have helped me. I didn't pass the Eleven Plus and was assigned to Secondary Modern School.

At that point I vowed that I would become a teacher, find children like myself and others that had learning difficulties, and help them.

I had to work hard to achieve what others take for granted, but I made it. The Principal of my teaching college told me, 'Your spelling is appalling but you are a gifted teacher and if you promise to always work with a diary by your side I'm going to trust myself and let you pass.' I am proud to say my teaching certificate states, 'With distinction in practical teaching'. I have spent all my teaching life keeping that promise.

When my children arrived I spent three years studying with the Open University and became more knowledgeable about child development and how children learn.

Later when my children were teenagers I studied for a Diploma in Education at Exeter University, and once again added to my knowledge of children with reading and writing difficulties. My own dissertation included research into word-finding difficulties, especially using different coloured backgrounds and coloured fonts. I also worked with putting coloured gels on spectacles. I hope my research added to our knowledge of how the brain preserves the written language.

If you look at the pages in this book you will notice that they aren't printed on white paper but on 'buff', a slightly yellow tone (in my experimenting I noted that blue text on a creamy yellow was so much easier for all readers).

My first attempt at a recipe book was to photocopy my favourite recipes, staple them together, and sell them for 20 pence a copy for school funds. At the time I was a Headteacher, very busy, and usually trying to fundraise, so selling my recipes seemed a good idea.

I called it 'Friday Treats' because every Thursday evening I would bake for my family and staff, and take the treat into school on Friday morning. Then I'd invite the staff to join me in the staff room and have a cuppa. I knew I could never pay them for all the extras they did, but I could show my appreciation by baking for them with love.

I've gone on batch-baking in large quantities ever since. This has stood me in good stead not just for my schools, but also for all sorts of fundraising, mostly for charity events. It's something I still love to do; and of course at home if you make large quantities, it means you can have some delicious treats standing by in your freezer.

Something else that is little known about me is that before I went on Bake Off, I'd had a life-threatening accident. I have osteoporosis, and I had a bad fall, breaking three bones in my left hand, and also my right humerus. I needed serious surgery and blood transfusions, and it was a long painful recovery; my whole kitchen had to be rebuilt so that I could reach things easily. As I recovered I took stock of my life and decided I needed to do some things like walk on the Great Wall of China, and that I should pass on recipes and tips to the next generation and do something extraordinary. That's why I applied to go on Bake Off.

I am a great advocate of a healthy lifestyle, I went to a gym for almost thirty years, and Physical Education was one of my specialisms (hence the stepping as I bake). After the accident it took me more than a year to have the courage to run again in case I fell and broke more bones. Now I 'wobble'; to be precise, I run 100 paces and fast-walk 100 paces; not the best style but it keeps me moving and fit.

Baking is quite a sedentary activity so I have devised ways of exercising as I bake. One trick is that I keep the majority of my ingredients upstairs in a spare bedroom so as I bake I have to go up and down stairs many times.

I put on my favourite upbeat music to give me a motivational lift to move; it's amazing how many side steps you can fit in as you beat the mixture for your Victoria Sponge (500), rub in butter for scones or pastry (200), or make lemon curd (1,000 and a bit of a dance if you feel like it)!

I have always followed a healthy balanced diet, the operative word being 'balanced'. I see no harm in a weekly treat, and personally if I indulge in something high in fat, calories and sugar, I make sure it's a treat and not a daily routine. I really do feel that 'everything in moderation' is a good motto. It's fine to eat the occasional 'naughty but nice' treat but balance it out with healthy options on other days.

And talking of health, I know there is a need to provide bakes for all sorts of different requirements: gluten-free, vegan, lactose-free, and egg-free, as well as fat-free and sugar-free. I have included recipes where adaptations can easily be made. In most of the recipes you can substitute gluten-free flour for ordinary flour, and it's worth experimenting with different ingredients until you get your own perfect bake.

I have baked for more than fifty years and been a full-time working mum for forty, collecting recipes and devising my own. The ones that have stood the test of time are those that are quick and simple to make and always please. It is these bakes that I want to share with you.

American friends

JoAnne Cortese, manager of Pain d'Avignon, compiled the list below!

Some of the ingredients I've used may be unfamiliar in America. When I was there, I found most things by going online. British brands, such as McVitie's, Lyle's Golden Syrup, Lyle's Dark Treacle, Birds Custard and Colman's English Mustard Powder, can usually be found on Amazon, World Market and British Food Depot, though you can substitute American equivalents (see below).

You'll probably need to check online for mixed spice, demerara sugar, cassia extract, chocolate extract, rose water, rose syrup, rose jam, glycerine and sultanas. Glacé cherries can be found on Nuts.com and Amazon or you can use candied cherries.

You can get Double cream from Whole Foods Market or online. Likewise, rapeseed oil can sometimes be found in health food stores.

I used King Arthur's Flour (kingarthurflour.com), they have a good range of flours and gluten-free flours, and they also have a selection of extracts and a good Dutch cocoa powder.

Unwaxed lemons and oranges are rarely found in America, so the best thing to do is put them in boiling water to loosen the wax, then take them out and scrub with a vegetable brush.

Here's a list of British/American equivalents:

BRITISH	AMERICAN
Barley wine	This is pale ale, use a US version, around 5% alcohol by volume
Black treacle	US light molasses (not blackstrap) is the nearest equivalent
Cassia	Nearest equivalent is probably cinnamon, you'll need to use less
Caster sugar	Superfine sugar. Make your own by whizzing regular cane sugar in a food processor
Demarara sugar	Your best bet may be Turbinado sugar, though it won't give the same crunchy finish
Digestive biscuits	Graham crackers
Double cream	Heavy cream

BRITISH	AMERICAN
Elderflower liqueur	St. Germain Elderflower Liquor
Glacé cherries	Candied cherries
Glycerine	Glycerin, or use corn oil
Golden syrup	You could substitute corn syrup
Icing sugar	Confectioner's sugar
Maris Piper potatoes	Idaho Russet or other floury potatoes
Rapeseed oil	Substitute this with another vegetable oil with low saturated fat
Rolled oats	Regular oats
Sultanas	White or golden raisins

Baking equipment

A set or two of good digital scales are essential – always keep spare batteries. The reason I have two sets is because sometimes in the middle of a baking session my scales run out of power, so I use a second set, and sort batteries out later.

Here is a tip about using your scales. In order to bake perfect cupcakes, place your baking tray on your weighing scales and set it to zero. Then you can weigh out exact quantities of cake mixture and zero the scales between each cupcake.

Measuring spoons: I have 3 sets; I collect interesting ones, and it saves me having to wash spoons mid-bake.

A set of measuring cups; I have a stainless steel set. A lot of American recipes are given in cups, though I prefer the more accurate method of weight in grams.

I have a huge number of baking tins/pans for every occasion, which I have built up over time.

2 flat baking sheets with no raised edges; this makes it easier to lift biscuits, scones and cookies off the tray when baked.

When I first met my husband's grandma, she used cast iron pans and baking sheets for everything, and she baked on a Yorkshire range, with a coal fire that heated two ovens to the side. Grandma Hetherington taught me how to judge the temperature by placing a piece of brown paper on the oven shelf for two minutes. If it went deep brown around the edges, it was hot enough for pastry and scones. Last year I approached the Netherton Foundry to design and make me a cast iron baking sheet, so you can now buy 'Val's Baking Sheet'. For every tray sold, we donate £2 to the Multiple Sclerosis Society.

A heavy-duty Swiss roll pan (I have two the same size for making a Christmas Yule log, and two more bigger ones for making large-scale Swiss rolls/jelly rolls/roulades).

2 tray bake pans, 23cm x 33cm.

2 brownie pans: 1 square 21cm, and one rectangular 23cm x 33cm.

4 sandwich round tins/pans 20cm diameter.

4 sandwich round tins/pans 23cm diameter.

2 springform loose-bottom round 23cm tins.

2 x 2lb loaf tins.

2 x 12-hole cupcake tins. These are deeper than bun tins and they can be used for smaller bun cases and help keep the shape of buns better.

2 x square 23cm loose-bottomed cake tins.

If you are cooking for large numbers, or want to freeze half of what you bake, it makes sense to bake 4 cakes at once, in which case you'll need four rather than two of each tin.

At least 2 large cooling racks; not the round ones as they waste space on your worktops.

Bundt tins; I've recently added a number of bundt tins to my collection. Most of my cake recipes can be made in a bundt tin.

Parchment, silicone liners, bun cases and grease-proof baking tin liners. These save a lot of time whenever the recipe says 'line and grease'! Here is what I use:

A roll of baking parchment to line tray bake tins and Swiss roll tins.

4-6 silicone non-stick baking mats that can be put on baking sheets for biscuits, scones and pastries; these are also ideal for baking meringues and macaroons.

I use Bake-O-Glide silicone sheets, which I cut to fit my trays and the bottoms and sides of cake baking tins. I use the off-cuts to line a brownie pan or mini loaf tins, and I use a small piece on my scales when I'm weighing, to save having to wash the whole scales.

For macaroons and individual meringues, silicone liners with circles printed on them give perfect piping guidance.

Buy good cupcake cases; I find that the foil ones made by Wilton are expensive but good, because they don't come away from the cakes after a day or so.

If you are going to make cupcakes regularly, you might want cupcake carriers which carry 12 cupcakes. They clip together to make it easy to transport the cakes safely. Also you can buy pretty packs to sell cupcakes in.

Invest in a large and a small offset palette knife as these are the best tools for lifting items from baking trays and for spreading buttercream and cream.

I find that cellophane bags, raffia and pretty string are all useful for wrapping cupcakes, biscuits and other baked goods for cake stalls, fund-raising events and all sorts of other occasions.

I have a stand-mixer and a hand-held mixer, both of which I think are indispensable, but of course it is perfectly possible to mix by hand, as I used to do when I was a child, baking with my mum.

Also I have a microwave, which I find useful for melting butter or chocolate, but you can use a double-boiler or a heat-proof bowl over a pan of simmering water, which does the job just as well though it takes a little longer.

Icing requirements

Piping bags: you can buy disposable bags, which save time; a large size for a big batch of icing and a smaller size for smaller jobs. When you have finished you can cut the end off by the nozzle and throw away the bag. If ethically this doesn't sit well, buy 2 large and 2 small nylon piping bags.

There are hundreds of piping nozzles on the market, but start simply with the following and add to your collection as you become more adventurous:

A Wilton 6 point star (2D) which makes good-looking stars and roses.

A larger 6 point star (844).

A plain round nozzle (2cm diameter) for piping on top of cupcakes.

A fine round nozzle for writing with royal icing and buttercream and for doing fine details.

This list of requirements isn't a definitive list, but I hope it will get you started.

Basic kitchen ingredients

My family and friends make jokes about the quantities of ingredients I keep in my home. They suggest that if there is a public emergency, they will move in with me because I have enough staples to keep several families going for months. It is a habit I got into before we could order online; I would shop once a month, being a working mum who needed to be organised and save time. Now I do a monthly online shop and save myself the need to physically carry staples such as flour, sugar and other heavy ingredients.

The following list roughly represents my monthly online order.

Flours

I tend to buy 2 bags of each flour: plain, self-raising, white bread-making flour, gluten-free plain, gluten-free self-raising, and baking powder (Dr Oetkers is gluten-free). It's worth experimenting with gluten-free flours; they are suitable for most of the recipes.

I also keep dried yeast in my cupboard but I buy fresh yeast online and it keeps for a month or can be frozen. If you go to the bread-making section in your local supermarket and ask nicely they will usually let you have a piece of fresh yeast.

Sugars

At least 1kg each of granulated, caster, light brown, dark brown, icing sugar and Demerara. I like to use unrefined or organic sugars if I can. For golden caster sugar, I use Billington's.

As a natural brown sugar alternative, I use Sukrin Gold, which is based on stevia.

A squeezy bottle of golden syrup can be poured in a controlled way, more easily than using a tin.

Fats

I buy 8 blocks of butter at a time and freeze what I don't use immediately. I prefer to buy unsalted Lurpac or Le President as these have less water than other butters.

I buy a big 2kg tub of soft Stork margarine, which works really well in most recipes, especially all-in-one Victoria sponge; you can also buy it in the smaller 500g tubs.

You will need a litre bottle of sunflower oil, and the same of olive oil, plus a smaller quantity of groundnut oil and coconut oil.

Eggs

I buy at least 2 dozen (24) each week but you may need fewer. I have included some egg-free recipes and also a few egg substitutes.

Weight of eggs out of shells:
1 large egg = 50g
White only = 30g
Yolk only = 18g
2 eggs = 60g white and 36g yolk
3 eggs = 90g white and 54g yolk

Pasteurised egg whites can be bought in cartons, which is easier than having egg yolks left over.

Egg allergy and vegan needs

Sometimes you need to substitute another ingredient for eggs. For me this began when my dad had heart surgery and I wanted to reduce his egg intake. Here are some alternatives; choose what suits the flavours in the recipe.

Apple sauce (match the weight of the eggs in the recipe or use a quarter cup per egg)

Mashed bananas (match the weight of the eggs in the recipe or use a quarter cup per egg)

Ground chia or flax seeds (1 egg = 1 tablespoon of ground seeds plus 1 tablespoon of water)

Sunflower oil (match the weight of the eggs in the recipe or use a quarter cup per egg).

Do not use the oil substitute for a cake needing more than one egg (two at most) as it will make the bake too oily.

I have used a quarter cup of oil, 2 tablespoons of water and 2 teaspoons of baking powder in cakes and cookies to replace an egg, and this works well; folk say they can't tell that there isn't any egg in the recipe.

Cake making

Below is a list of items that will last for months.

Flavours and extracts (I prefer extracts as they have a strong natural flavour): vanilla extract, vanilla paste, almond extract, lemon extract, orange extract, rose extract, coffee extract, chocolate extract.

Holy Lama Spice Drops are concentrated extracts for bakes, cooking and drinks. They have a shelf life of three years and have won several Great Taste awards. I use liquid cinnamon, ginger, cardamom and others.

Food colours: buy gel colours in a tube as they are easy to squeeze a drop at a time, and save messing with a cocktail stick.

Cooking chocolate: I use Callebaut, both 70.5% and 54% cocoa, usually the 2.5 kg bag of chocolate chips; they melt quickly and evenly.

Cocoa: I use Rowntrees or Dr Oetker fine dark cocoa powder.

Spices

You will need to keep a stock of basic spices: ground cinnamon and cinnamon sticks, ground ginger and whole nutmegs.

Spice drops: liquid cinnamon, ginger, cardamom, and more.

Nuts

If your cakes include nuts, you might want to add a 'Contains nuts' label if you are making large quantities for the public.

Quantities for baking

If you are baking for large numbers, double the quantities of ingredients in recipes. If you do bake large amounts, you will find that nearly all these cakes and bakes can be frozen, and I tell you in the recipes how long they can stay in the freezer.

US equivalents

When I spent time baking in America I had to replace UK ingredients with US ones. In America I usually shop at Williams's and Sonoma or Crate and Barrel, or I shop online. For all my many American friends, you might like to look at page 9 for further information on US equivalents to British brands.

Chantilly cream

INGREDIENTS

500ml double cream

1 tablespoon dried milk powder

1-2 heaped tablespoons icing sugar

1 teaspoon of vanilla extract or vanilla paste or 1 teaspoon extract required by the recipe

If making a flavoured cream

3 tablespoons of liqueur or cordial as required

3 tablespoons lemon/lime curd, fruit purée or crushed soft fruits

METHOD

1. Chill your mixing bowl and beaters before making the cream. Use a stand or a hand electric mixer if you have one.
2. Place the double cream in the bowl with the dried milk and let stand for a minute to allow the powder to dissolve in the cream.
3. Beat the cream on medium power for 1 minute.
4. Add the icing sugar and any flavour extract, and beat on medium until the cream begins to form floppy peaks.
5. Gradually add any cordial or liqueurs in a steady stream and beat on slow until blended, then beat on medium until the cream forms slightly firm peaks.
6. For a flavoured cream, fold in lemon or lime curd, fruit purée or crushed fruit. If you intend to pipe with the cream, leave about one third without fruit added as this will block the piping nozzle.
7. Place in the fridge until needed.

Buttercream

I always use a good quality unsalted butter. Adding a little cream cheese helps the buttercream not taste too sweet. Sufficient for a 3-tier 23cm round cake, or a similar tray bake or 12 cupcakes.

INGREDIENTS

200g unsalted butter at room temperature

600g icing sugar, sifted

50g cream cheese

flavourings and colourings as required

METHOD

1. Place the butter in a chilled stand bowl or large mixing bowl and beat for 2 minutes.
2. Add the other ingredients and beat for 10 minutes until light and fluffy.

Chocolate buttercream

INGREDIENTS

100g plain chocolate chips (70% cocoa butter)

1 tablespoon of water

60g unsalted butter

50g cocoa powder

150g icing sugar sifted

1 egg yolk

METHOD

1. Place the the chocolate and water in a heavy pan, stirring continuously until melted, then set aside to cool slightly.
2. Beat the butter, cocoa powder and icing sugar until light and fluffy.
3. Beat in the egg yolk and then the melted chocolate. If the icing is a little slack add another 1-2 tablespoons of icing sugar. It will cool to a thicker consistency.

Royal icing

This can be used for icing biscuits and cookies.

INGREDIENTS

40g egg white (1-2 egg whites)

half a teaspoon of lemon juice for a firm icing

or half a teaspoon glycerine to keep the icing soft

250g icing sugar

flavouring and colourings as required

METHOD

1. Using either a hand electric mixer or a stand mixer if you have one, lightly beat the egg whites with the lemon juice or the glycerine.
2. Sieve the icing sugar and add half to the egg whites. Beat well.
3. Add the remainder of the icing sugar a tablespoon at a time until the icing is stiff enough to stand in peaks.
4. Add flavours and colours as required by the recipe.

Glacé icing

This thin icing can be drizzled over cakes or cookies to add a little extra sweetness.

INGREDIENTS

100g sieved icing sugar

15ml warm water

flavourings and colourings as required

METHOD

1. Place the icing sugar in a bowl, add the water and stir until smooth.
2. Add flavourings and colourings and stir well until all combined.
3. Use immediately as this icing will dry out quickly.
4. If you need to leave the icing for a few minutes, dampen a tea towel and place over the bowl of icing until required.

Salted caramel

Caramel can be eaten as a topping on ice cream or yoghurt but it can also be added to brownies or other cakes to make them sublime.

INGREDIENTS

200g granulated sugar

60ml water

50g salted butter

150ml double cream

½ teaspoon fine sea salt

Salted caramel sauce can be kept at room temperature for up to three days or refrigerated for up to four weeks.

METHOD

1 Heat three jam jars in a warm oven while you make the sauce.

2 Place the sugar and the water In a medium-heavy saucepan.

3 Bring to the boil, shaking the pan until the sugar has dissolved.

4 Use a wet pastry brush to push undissolved sugar crystals from the sides into the pan. This prevents crystals forming in the caramel.

5 When the mixture reaches a boil, allow it to boil until it turns a deep amber colour; don't let it burn.

6 Throughout the boiling time, continue to shake the pan occasionally so that it cooks evenly.

7 Add the butter and whisk vigorously until melted. Continue to boil for one minute, keeping well back as the mixture will bubble and spit.

8 Remove the pan from the heat and gently pour in the cream. It will bubble up as before so be careful!

9 Stir the mixture until combined and add the salt.

10 Transfer the salted caramel to the warmed jam jars and allow to cool uncovered at room temperature, then cover.

Apricot glaze

This glaze gives a cake a lovely sheen and colour.

INGREDIENTS

2 tablespoons apricot jam

2 tablespoons water

METHOD

1 Place the jam and water in a heavy pan and bring to boil.

2 Put the mixture through a sieve before brushing on the cake while the glaze is still warm.

Lemon/ lime/ orange drizzle

INGREDIENTS

200g icing sugar

juice of 2 lemons

METHOD

1 Place in a pan and stir to dissolve the sugar, bring the mixture to simmering point and allow to simmer for 5 minutes to reduce the drizzle.

Condensed milk caramel

INGREDIENTS

I-4 tin(s) condensed milk

METHOD 1

1 Place the unopened tin(s) of condensed milk in a slow cooker and add water to just cover.

2 Set the cooker to the lowest setting and simmer for 8 hours or overnight.

3 When cool remove the tin(s) and with a permanent marker pen write 'caramel' on the top. The caramel will retain the 'use by' date of the condensed milk.

METHOD 2

4 Place a pan on the hob large enough to take 2-4 tins of condensed milk side by side.

5 Add boiling water to the pan to cover the tins, place a lid on the pan and simmer for 3 hours.

6 The tins must always be covered; top up with boiling water when needed.

7 Continue simmering for another 3 hours with the lid removed.

8 Allow the tins to cool in the pan. Remove and label as before.

Cream cheese frosting

Ideal for carrot cake and cupcakes, it's not as sweet as buttercream. This is enough to fill and decorate a cake, tray bake or 12 cupcakes

INGREDIENTS

50g unsalted butter

400g cream cheese

zest, flavourings and colourings as required

200g icing sugar

METHOD

1 Place the butter and cream cheese in a bowl and beat until combined.

2 Add the the zest, flavourings and colourings.

3 Add the icing sugar a dessert spoon at a time until all combined, beat for 8-10 minutes until light and fluffy.

4 Place in the fridge for an hour to allow the frosting to harden a little before removing and cutting into pieces.

Marmalade with
Cointreau
26.11.17

20
270
188

Tray bakes

My mum was a great fan of tray bakes. There were four of us hungry children in the family, and cutting a round cake could often start squabbles as to who was getting the biggest piece. When Mum made square cakes, she found it was easier to serve, though it didn't quite eliminate the squabbles.

Tray bakes are easier to decorate too, no sides to think about!

Like a lot of recipes in this book, tray bakes are ideal for charity bakes and any other occasions when you're catering for large numbers. They're also easy to transport.

They can be made in foil trays and sold as a whole or in slices. And of course, you can freeze them; rectangular or square boxes take up the least space in the freezer.

INGREDIENTS

230g golden syrup

250g unsalted butter chopped into cubes plus extra for greasing the baking trays

380g chocolate (chocolate chips melt easily)

2 x 500g packets chocolate biscuits (milk or plain, or simple digestive biscuits or graham crackers)

100g mini marshmallows

Topping

50g M&Ms

50g plain chocolate

Rocky roads

Makes approximately 12–16
Preparation 15 minutes, setting 2 hours

When we had fund-raising events at school, my kind parents would bring in their delicious bakes. Rocky roads were always popular and over the years I have developed the recipe to be as simple or as luxurious as I want. This recipe is the basic one but you can make it special with a few additional ingredients. My personal choice is to use chocolate digestives and you can use gluten-free biscuits if you prefer.

METHOD

1. Place golden syrup, cubed butter and chocolate in a microwaveable bowl. Microwave for 1 minute, stir and repeat twice more or until the ingredients have melted and combined. Alternatively, heat in a pan until melted.
2. Meanwhile, place the biscuits in a large plastic bag and seal. Use a rolling pin to crush the biscuits not too small, leaving some larger pieces. If you are using cream biscuits they will stick a little bit. Scrape the cream into the mixture; it will be fine.
3. Pour the crushed biscuits into a large bowl.
4. Add the golden syrup mixture and stir in well until all combined.
5. Add the marshmallows and stir in well.
6. Prepare a baking tray 30cm x 23cm and 4cm deep, pour in the biscuit mixture and use a palette knife to level it off.
7. Sprinkle on the M&Ms and press them into the biscuit mixture and leave to set.
8. Place the 50g plain chocolate in a small bowl and microwave on medium heat for 2 bursts of 1 minute, or melt in a pan over boiling water.
9. Before all the chocolate has melted, stir until it's completely melted. It's not exactly tempering chocolate but it does give it a shine.
10. Use a piping bag to drizzle chocolate over the top of the Rocky roads.
11. Allow to set hard before cutting into squares or rectangles.
12. For a smooth chocolate topping, omit the M&Ms and instead of 50g of chocolate use 200g of chocolate. Once melted, pour over the bake and smooth out evenly.
13. When it's set (about 2 hours), cut into pieces and store in an airtight box; they will keep well for three weeks or you can freeze them for up to six weeks.

Variations

Most biscuits work for this recipe, including gluten-free ones. I vary the chocolate, dark or milk depending on what I have in the house. You can add different kinds of 'rubble' into the mix: smarties, chocolate chips or chunks – be creative and see what you come up with.

The flapjack needs to be cut while it is warm. If you leave it to cool completely, it will break into small pieces, in which case store in a box as these are lovely crumbled over yoghurt and fruit.

M&M flapjacks

Makes 24
Preparation 15 minutes, cooking 30-40 minutes

The original version of this flapjack recipe is in the Hamlyn All Colour Cook Book, first printed in 1970 (I bought my copy in 1978). Mary Berry wrote the baking section and I loved her recipes. When I was on Bake Off she very kindly signed my copy. Over the years I have developed the recipe to include lots of different ingredients but M&Ms are the all-time winner. The addition of cinnamon adds warmth and the vanilla helps the chocolate come through.

INGREDIENTS

454g soft margarine

900g golden syrup

140g granulated sugar

920g rolled oats plus about 100g if the mixture looks too loose

1 teaspoon fine sea salt

½ teaspoon ground cinnamon

2 teaspoons vanilla extract

70g mini M&Ms, plus 30g for the topping

Optional

1 unwaxed orange

or chopped apricots

or chocolate chips

METHOD

1. Set the oven to 150°C fan, 160°C, 335°F, mark 3.
2. Grease a baking pan with a little butter.
3. Put the margarine and syrup in a pan and place on a low heat until the margarine has melted. Or microwave on medium setting for 2 minutes.
4. In a bowl place the sugar, oats, salt and cinnamon and combine.
5. Add the vanilla extract to the syrup mixture, pour onto the oat mixture and mix thoroughly.
6. Stir in the M&Ms.
7. Turn the mixture into the pan and press down well with a spatula. Scatter the remaining M&Ms evenly on the top.
8. Bake for 30-40 minutes until golden brown.
9. Leave to cool in the tin for 5 minutes, then using a sharp knife, cut into 24 pieces.
10. Leave for another 2 minutes before lifting out (you may need to cut into pieces again if the flapjack feels as though it may break when lifting out). Place on a wire cooling rack and leave until completely cold.

Store in an airtight tin, or freeze. The flapjacks will keep for four weeks and you can freeze them for up to two months.

Variations

Add raisins or sultanas soaked in the zest and juice of an unwaxed orange until all the juice is soaked into the fruit. Experiment with your favourite flavours, perhaps adding chopped apricots or chocolate chips, or whatever takes your fancy.

Marmalade
Cointreau
26.11.17

Sticky orange flapjack

Makes 14-18
Preparation 10 minutes, cooking 25-30 minutes

I fell in love with this recipe more than 15 years ago. One of my lovely home-baking mums made it for a school sale and the tangy orange contrasted with the golden syrup so perfectly that I decided to have a go myself. I added my own twist, making them totally moreish: a hint of cinnamon and a dash of vanilla.

INGREDIENTS

- zest and juice of 2 unwaxed medium-sized oranges
- 250g unsalted butter, cut into small pieces
- 250g golden caster sugar
- 170g golden syrup
- 450g porridge oats
- ½ teaspoon cinnamon
- ½ teaspoon vanilla extract
- 50g sunflower seeds or mixed seeds (sunflower, pumpkin, linseed, and sesame seeds)
- 100g fine shredded orange marmalade

METHOD

1. Set the oven to 160°C fan, 180-190°C, 350-375°F, gas 4-5.
2. Squeeze the juice from half an orange and set aside.
3. Using a citrus zester, remove the zest and place in a heavy-based pan (or in a microwaveable bowl).
4. Add the butter, sugar and syrup.
5. Melt the ingredients on a medium heat, or in the microwave on medium, until the butter has melted.
6. Remove from the heat and stir in the oats, cinnamon and vanilla until the oats are combined well with the other ingredients.
7. Turn the mixture into a prepared baking tin and use an offset spatula to level off the surface.
8. Scatter the seeds over the mixture.
9. Place in the oven and bake for 25-30 minutes. It is ready when the edges are golden brown but the middle remains a little soft.
10. Leave in the tin until almost cold.
11. Put the marmalade and water in a pan and warm through to make a syrup.
12. Brush the syrup evenly over the flapjack, turn the flapjack out onto a board and cut into 14, 16 or 18 pieces.

Store in an airtight container for up to a week, or freeze for up to two months.

INGREDIENTS

For the tray bake

450g soft light brown sugar

375ml sunflower oil

5 large eggs (320g out of their shells)

225g self-raising flour

14g ground mixed spice

2g ground cinnamon

a pinch fine sea salt

380g grated carrot

185g pecans

120g sultanas

grated zest of one unwaxed orange (save the juice for the syrup)

1 teaspoon vanilla extract

For the orange syrup

juice of one whole orange

40g caster sugar

For the buttercream frosting

200g unsalted butter

100g full-fat cream cheese

600g icing sugar

finely grated zest and juice of an unwaxed orange

1 teaspoon orange extract

120g of caramelised pecan halves, if you can find them

Carrot cake tray bake

Makes 16-24
Preparation 30 minutes, baking 40-50 minutes, decorating 20 minutes

My friend Louise gave me a carrot cake recipe more than twenty years ago and I have added ingredients and made it a family favourite. I always made it in a round tin until I saw Jo Wheatley making hers as a tray bake, which makes it much easier to cut. It's also part of your 5-a-day with carrots, sultanas and nuts, and is made with vegetable oil. I need to thank Jo Wheatley again for something that makes this recipe even more special: the addition of an orange syrup that ensures the cake stays really moist. To lower the calories you might want to halve the amount of buttercream topping!

METHOD

1. Set the oven to 160°C fan, 180-190°C, 350-375°F, gas 4-5.
2. Prepare a rectangular shallow baking tin 30cm x 23cm, or a round 20cm-diameter deep baking tin.
3. Place the sugar and oil in the mixer bowl and mix well until all combined and smooth.
4. Break the eggs into a bowl and beat lightly. Add slowly to the sugar mixture and beat until smooth.
5. Sift the flour, spices, salt into a bowl, then with a metal tablespoon fold into the oil mixture. Fold in the grated carrot, pecans, orange zest, orange extract, vanilla extract and sultanas.
6. Pour the mixture into the baking tin and tap the tin on the work surface to level off.
7. Place in the oven on the middle shelf and bake for 40-50 minutes.
8. Check the cake after 40 minutes; it should be golden and firm to touch, and a skewer should come out cleanly if inserted in the middle of the cake. If you lift the cake to your ear it should hardly be making a sound, no crackling from any mixture still cooking inside the cake.

For the orange syrup

9. Place the orange juice and sugar in a small pan, swirl the pan over the heat to help dissolve the sugar and bring to a steady boil; then reduce the heat and simmer until the syrup is reduced by one third.
10. When the cake is baked, remove it from the oven and brush with the warm syrup; place the tin on a cooling rack and leave to go completely cold.
11. For the buttercream filling, use the quantities given here and follow the recipe on page 14.
12. To decorate the cake spread the frosting evenly over the top and scatter with the pecans.
13. Place in the fridge for an hour to allow the frosting to harden a little before removing and cutting into pieces. Serve the cake from the tray or store the cut pieces in boxes (use a piece of baking parchment to cover the first layer and then stack the pieces two deep without spoiling the topping).

This cake will keep for a week in an airtight container or will freeze well for two months.

Instead of raisins try a mixture of dried fruits such as apricots, cherries or cranberries or a little of each to equal the quantity of dried fruit in the recipe.

Makes 6 large or 8 small wedges
Preparation 15 minutes, setting 2-3 hours

This nut, fruit, chocolate and biscuit treat is my take on tiffin. When my children were little they would sing the Cadbury's advert song because it reminded them of a Cadbury's fruit and nut chocolate bar. It's a perfect after-dinner treat if served as a thin wedge, as the dark chocolate isn't sweet; the sweetness comes from the raisins. You can use either a round tin or a rectangular brownie tin.

Fruity chocolate tiffin wedges

INGREDIENTS

230g crushed digestive biscuits (or gluten-free biscuits)

250g dark 70% chocolate (save 50g of the chocolate to melt on the top of the tiffin)

55g unsalted butter, diced into cm cubes

50g/2 tablespoons clear honey

1 teaspoon vanilla extract

100g raisins

50g walnuts or pecans broken into small pieces

METHOD

1. Grease a 20cm round springform cake tin, or a brownie tin.
2. Place the biscuits in a plastic bag, seal with a wire twist, and use the rolling pin to crush the biscuits into small crumbs. Set aside.
3. Place 200g of the chocolate in a microwaveable bowl with the butter and microwave on low for 3 one-minute bursts, taking out and stirring after each minute (or melt in a pan over low heat).
4. When the butter and chocolate are melted, add the honey and vanilla extract and stir well.
5. Stir in the raisins and nuts.
6. Lastly stir in the biscuit crumbs and combine all well. Pour the mixture into the tin or tin and press down evenly and firmly.
7. Place in the fridge to set for about an hour.
8. Melt the remaining 50g of chocolate in the microwave for 3 bursts of one minute on a low setting, or melt over low heat in a small pan. When melted spread evenly over the tiffin and allow to set thoroughly before cutting into wedges or squares.

These are best kept in the fridge but brought out at least 15 minutes before serving to allow them to come to room temperature.

Variation

Try using milk chocolate for this recipe.

Millionaire's shortcake

Makes 16-20
Preparation 10 minutes, baking 25 minutes, caramel 30 minutes, topping 10 minutes

I've been making this recipe for many years; it's a children's party favourite and I haven't met an adult with a sweet tooth who could resist this bake. It cuts neatly when baked and is ideal for large numbers as well as family.

INGREDIENTS

For the shortcake

500g self-raising flour

350g margarine

175g caster sugar

For the caramel

115g caster sugar

115g margarine

225g golden syrup

2 small tins of condensed milk

For the chocolate topping

350g chocolate chips either milk or dark

115g white chocolate chips

METHOD

To make the shortcake

1. Set the oven to 160°C fan, 180-190°C, 350-375°F, gas 4-5.
2. Grease a 24cm x 33cm tray bake tin.
3. Place the flour and margarine in a large bowl and rub in the fat until it forms crumbs, then stir in the sugar.
4. Pour the crumb mixture into the tin, spreading to the edges.
5. Bake in the middle of the oven for 20-25 minutes until lightly golden and slightly firm to touch. It will continue to firm up as it cools.
6. Set aside to cool while you make the caramel.

To make the caramel

7. Dissolve the sugar, margarine, golden syrup and condensed milk in a heavy pan over heat; stir briskly continuously to ensure all the ingredients combine.
8. Bring the mixture up to a steady boil where it bubbles gently and not fiercely. Continue to stir as the caramel can easily burn.
9. If a few darkened pieces of caramel appear, just make sure you stir every bit of the bottom of the pan. The caramel will continue to turn golden and you will hardly notice the darker bits.
10. After 25 minutes take the pan off the heat and test to see if the caramel has reached setting point. It is set when you coat the back of a wooden spoon with caramel and draw the end of a knife through it to leave a channel which doesn't close up. If the caramel runs back, place the pan back on the heat and continue to stir for another 5 minutes, then test again.
11. When the caramel is set, pour it straightaway over the shortcake, lift the tray up and tilt it to allow the caramel to run to the corners and around the edges. Be careful, the caramel is boiling hot.
12. When the caramel is spread completely, tap the tray on the work surface to level out, place on a cooling rack and allow to cool completely before adding the chocolate layer.

To make the chocolate layer

13. Melt most of the milk or dark chocolate chips in a pan over boiling water, or in a double boiler, or microwave on medium/low for three one-minute bursts, stirring well between bursts. Stir continuously until the chips have melted, then add the remaining chips and stir in until completely melted – they will cool the mixture down, a simple chocolate tempering technique.
14. Pour the chocolate over the caramel and quickly spread with a spatula to cover, tap the tray down on the work surface several times to level out the chocolate.
15. Quickly melt most of the white chocolate as above. Stir in the remaining unmelted white chocolate chips until completely dissolved.
16. Place a small icing bag with a small nozzle in a small straight tumbler, pour in the white chocolate, then drizzle the white chocolate over the caramel in circles and zigzag patterns. Use a skewer to push the chocolate around in swirls.
17. If you feel more adventurous, try creating a herringbone effect by piping the white chocolate in horizontal lines across the bake (keeping the long side of the bake towards you). Then, starting at the far edge, dip the tip of a skewer in the chocolate, and pull towards you through the piped parallel lines of white chocolate. Move the skewer about 2 cm along and place in the dark chocolate again, on the side closest to you. Push the skewer away from you to the far edge of the tray. You will see the herringbone pattern appear; repeat along the bake. It's worth mastering this as it gives a very smart look to the bake.
18. Leave the Millionaire's shortcake to become completely cold before cutting.
19. Use a very sharp knife that has been dipped in boiling water and then dried, to cut into 16-24 pieces.
20. If a whiteish bloom appears on the chocolate, don't worry, dust with icing sugar so it disappears.

You can replace the glacé cherries with chocolate chips or mini chunks.

Cherry shortcake tray bake

Makes 12-16

Preparation 15 minutes, cooking 30-40 minutes

A long, long time ago I was given this recipe by a school cook; it made huge quantities and she did a very economical recipe using lard and margarine. I loved the recipe because it was so quick and easy. I exchanged the two fats for butter and liked it even more.

INGREDIENTS

375g unsalted butter

200g caster sugar plus extra for scattering over the top of the shortcake

1 teaspoon vanilla extract

570g plain flour

10g baking powder

175g glacé cherries

If the mixture sticks to the spatula, change to a fish slice dampened with a little water and continue until the shortcake is level and pressed down.

METHOD

1. Set the oven to 160°C fan, 180-190°C, 350-375°F, gas 4-5.
2. Grease a 24cm x 33cm tray bake tin.
3. Place the sugar, butter and vanilla extract in a bowl and beat until all combined but don't beat as much as you would for a Victoria sponge.
4. Sift the flour and baking powder into the butter mixture. Add the cherries so they get coated in a little flour, then fold the flour and cherries into the butter mixture until fully combined.
5. The mixture is quite a firm dough and will need dropping into the baking tin. With an offset spatula, push the mixture into the corners and level off so it will bake evenly; also press down so the finished bake will be firm and not too crumbly.
6. Place in the oven on the middle to bottom shelf, and bake for 30-40 minutes (if you are making a larger batch the timing will need adjusting to 40-50 minutes). Check to see if the shortcake is ready after 30 minutes, it should be turning golden around the edges but still pale in the middle and slightly firm to touch.
7. Give it 5 more minutes in the oven and keep doing this until it is ready to come out. The shortcake will continue to firm up as it cools, so place the baking tin on a cooling rack and allow the shortcake to cool completely before cutting.

Once cut, store the pieces in an airtight container where they will keep for a week or more depending on the weather. The shortcake freezes well for up to two months so if you are time-short but have an odd hour free at a weekend, bake a big batch and freeze them until needed. Allow them to defrost overnight on a worktop.

Mincemeat frangipane tart

INGREDIENTS

For the mincemeat

2 medium sized Bramley (cooking) apples around 150g when peeled

150g light brown sugar

150ml barley wine

zest and juice of 1 small orange

zest and juice of 1 small lemon

30g unsalted butter

100g raisins

25g pre-soaked Californian prunes, chopped

50g dried cherries, chopped

50g dried cranberries, chopped

150g sultanas

1 teaspoon mixed spice

½ teaspoon cinnamon

½ teaspoon freshly grated nutmeg

3 tablespoons brandy

3 tablespoons orange liqueur (or 6 tablespoons freshly squeezed orange juice)

Alternatively, use 1 x 822g jar or 2 x 410g jars of ready-made mincemeat.

For the sweet pastry

250g plain flour

100g icing sugar

100g unsalted butter

2 egg yolks

1 tsp water

For the frangipane

200g ground almonds

200g caster sugar

3 eggs

For finishing

caster sugar

flaked almonds

10 glacé cherries (halved)

Serves 8-10

Preparation: mincemeat one hour, pastry 15 minutes plus 1 hour chilling, cooking 40 minutes

My mum always bought her mincemeat for Christmas but when I started going out with my husband his mum and grandma taught me how to make it and I never bought it again. I usually make a huge batch and give lots away as gifts.

METHOD

To make the mincemeat

1 Peel and grate the apples and place in a large pan with the brown sugar, barley wine, zest and juice of the orange and lemon. Stir well and place on a medium heat. Gradually bring to the boil, stirring frequently until the apples are soft.

2 Add the butter, dried fruits and spices to the pan, stir well and simmer until thickened (30-40 minutes).

3 Remove from the heat and allow to cool completely. Once cool stir in the brandy and the orange liqueur, or the orange juice.

4 The mincemeat can be packed into jars or into fridge containers until needed.

To make the sweet pastry

5 Sift the flour and icing sugar together into a large bowl.

6 Rub in the butter until the mixture resembles fine breadcrumbs.

7 Add the egg yolks and water and work into a soft dough.

8 Form the dough into a ball. Wrap in clingfilm and place in the fridge for 30 minutes.

To make the frangipane

9 Combine the ingredients and mix them together until you have a dropping consistency.

Finishing

10 Set the oven to 160°C fan, 180-190°C, 350-375°F, gas 4-5

11 Prepare a loose-bottomed fluted round flan tin 23cm diameter or a shallow rectangular tin 30cm x 23cm.

12 Roll out the pastry and use it to line the greased tin. Gently push to fill the fluted edges. Prick the base of the pastry lightly.

13 Spread the mincemeat evenly on top of the pastry.

14 Layer the frangipane mixture on top of the mincemeat.

15 Decorate using caster sugar, flaked almonds or glacé cherries.

16 Bake for 40 minutes.

17 Sprinkle with icing sugar before serving.

Variation

For individual Bakewell tarts, make the pastry and cut 12 x 14.5cm fluted rounds, leave out the mincemeat but add a ¼ teaspoon jam into each tart, top with a teaspoon of frangipane mixture, scatter with caster sugar and flaked almonds, and bake for 15-20 minutes.

You can turn this into a single large Bakewell Tart by leaving out the mincemeat and instead spreading half a jar of raspberry jam on the pastry before topping with the frangipane as above.

Cupcake Day
Unedig Yn Erbyn Ddementia
United Against Dementia
Cupcake Day
Unedig Yn Erbyn Ddementia
United Against Dementia

Sirop
ΣΑΡΑΝΤΗΣ
ΤΡΙΑΝΤΑΦΥΛΛΟ

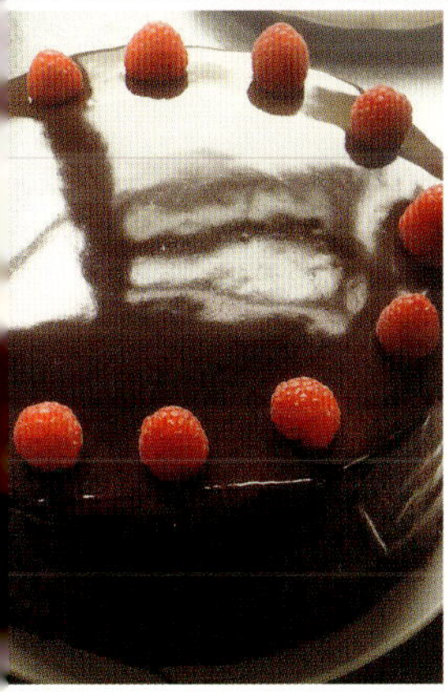

Cakes, cupcakes & muffins

Every single bake in this chapter has a history. Fruity mincemeat cake reminds me of cooking with my mother-in-law Val Stones (how good is that to have a mum-in-law with the same name!).

Baking Victoria sponge and rock cakes brings back recollections of Sunday baking with my mum. She always explained what she was doing and why, and she was taught in the same way by her mum, my Nana Heales.

Easter cupcakes revive memories of baking with my children, eating more chocolate eggs than we put on the cakes, and making the chicks hop onto the icing with the appropriate cheep-cheep noises.

Red velvet cupcakes remind me of my nephew Andrew in New York, who searched online to find me a recipe because I so enjoyed eating red velvety cupcakes while staying there.

HOME

Fruity mincemeat cake

Serves 8
Preparation: mincemeat 1 hour, cake 20 minutes, cooking 1-1¼ hours

My husband's mother-in-law taught me how to make this cake many years ago and her mother made it too. It's a quick and easy fruit cake, lighter than the usual Christmas cake and perfect if you have little time to soak fruit as the mincemeat adds lots of flavours and moisture. If you are really pushed for time you could use bought mincemeat.

INGREDIENTS

150g soft unsalted butter

150g light muscovado sugar

2 large eggs

225g self-raising flour, sifted

230g mincemeat (see pages 34-35 for a quick home-made recipe)

90g currants

110g sultanas

zest of a small unwaxed orange

½ teaspoon mixed spice

½ teaspoon cinnamon

50g blanched almonds, either split or whole (optional)

2 tablespoons sieved warm apricot jam (optional glaze)

METHOD

1. Set the oven to 160°C fan, 180°C, gas 4-5.
2. Line and grease 2 loaf tins or a round baking tin.
3. Place all the ingredients except the almonds in a large bowl and beat well until blended, about two minutes.
4. Turn into the prepared loaf tins or round tin.
5. Arrange the almonds neatly in rows on the loaf cakes or in a circular pattern on the round cake.
6. Bake for 1¼ hours or until golden brown and firm to touch.
7. After 1 hour check whether cooked by placing a skewer in the middle of the cake(s). When it comes out clean the cake(s) can be removed from the oven and placed on a cooling rack until completely cold before taking out of the tin.
8. You can glaze the top with warmed, sieved apricot jam while the cakes are warm.
9. Once cold, remove from the tins and store in an airtight container.

Unlike a rich fruit cake, this cake will need to be eaten within two weeks, that is if you can resist eating it all in one go!

Spiced apple cake

Serves 8
Preparation 25 minutes, baking 1 hour

I've been making this apple cake for twenty years; a friend gave me the basic recipe but I quickly adapted it. The addition of cinnamon and mixed spice adds warmth to the apples, which for me have to be Bramleys. I use both light and dark soft brown sugar which gives a rich, almost caramel, flavour to the cake. It's unusual in that it's a rubbed-in method. When making the cake, only 3 eggs are needed as the apples make the cake moist.

INGREDIENTS

350g self-raising flour (or gluten-free self-raising flour)

a pinch of salt

1 teaspoon mixed spice

½ teaspoon cinnamon

230g soft margarine

100g light soft brown sugar

70g dark soft brown sugar

120g sultanas

100ml cider or apple juice

500g cooking apples (peeled weight. Peel, core and dice the apples, saving half an apple to decorate the top of the cake). As you are preparing the apples, allow the diced apple to soak in the cider/apple juice, to absorb the juice

3 eggs

1 teaspoon vanilla extract

2 dessert spoons Demerara sugar

METHOD

1. Set the oven to 160°C fan, 180-190°C, 350-375°F, gas mark 4-5.
2. Line and grease a 2lb loaf tin or a 20cm or 23cm deep loose-bottomed tin.
3. Sift the flour, spices and salt into a large bowl.
4. Add the margarine to the flour in small pieces and rub in.
5. Stir in the sugars and the sultanas.
6. Stir in the diced apples.
7. Lightly beat the eggs and add the vanilla extract.
8. Fold the eggs into the mixture, do not beat.
9. Turn into the tin of your choice, smooth the top with a spoon and hollow out a little in the middle.
10. Sprinkle over the Demerara sugar and place the sliced apple down the middle of the cake.
11. Place on the middle shelf of the oven and bake for one hour, then check that the cake is baked by pushing a skewer into its middle. If it comes out clean then the cake can be taken out of the oven.
12. If you are using a loaf tin, let the cake cool for 5 minutes in the tin before lifting out and cooling completely on a cooling rack. If you are using a round cake tin allow to cool for 15 minutes before removing from the tin.

This cake can also be served warm with custard or with cream.

Try adding 3 tablespoons of marmalade instead of 100g of the apple.

In this recipe I'm using Somerset Miles tea and Somerset Sheppy's cider because I always like to support local producers. Wherever you live you can look out for local produce.

Serves 8
Preparation 30 minutes, cooking 80-90 minutes

My grandson Arthur 'helping' to ice a cake.

My mother-in-law taught me to make this cake, and when I got married it was the weekly cake that was used for packed lunches, afternoon visitors and always with a cuppa. Over the years I have developed it, but a cake can always be improved! I like to make it in a loaf tin as it cuts nicely into slices, but it also makes an excellent round cake.

Easy fruit cake

INGREDIENTS

300g mixed dried fruit (I use equal quantities of sultanas, raisins and currants)

100g light soft brown sugar or 50g each of light and dark soft brown sugar

100g unsalted butter/soft margarine

70ml of tea (make a pot of tea with 4 teabags and allow to brew for 5 minutes)

70ml dry cider, or 80ml water

2 tablespoons Calvados, whisky or brandy (optional)

2 medium eggs lightly beaten

zest of half an orange

1 rounded teaspoon of mixed spice

¼ teaspoon ground cinnamon

1 teaspoon vanilla extract

200g self-raising flour, sifted

50g glacé cherries, quartered

2 tablespoons apricot jam, warmed, to glaze the cake

METHOD

1. Set the oven to 155°C fan, 160°C, 300°F, gas 3.
2. Prepare 2 x 1lb loaf tins or a 2lb loaf tin or a 15-18cm round cake tin.
3. Place the fruit, sugar, margarine/butter, tea and cider in a microwaveable bowl and set the microwave to medium, microwave for 5 minutes and then stir well to combine all the ingredients. Repeat this twice more until the mixture is bubbling. Alternatively, bring these ingredients to the boil in a large pan and simmer for 15 minutes.
4. Remove from the heat and stir in the 2 tablespoons of alcohol.
5. Allow the fruit mixture to cool, then add the beaten egg, zest, spices and vanilla extract, and combine well.
6. Fold in the flour and lastly fold in the chopped cherries.
7. Turn the mixture into the baking tin(s).
8. Bake for 1½ hours. Check after 1 hour, by pushing a skewer into the middle of the cake; it will come out clean if the cake is baked; it should be golden and firm to touch.
9. Brush the top of the cake with the warmed apricot jam.
10. Allow the cake to cool in the tin for 10 minutes and then turn out onto a wire rack to cool completely.

When cool, store in an airtight container; this cake is best left for two to three days to mature before eating, or you can freeze for up to one month.

Virtuous cake

Vegan, lactose-free, egg-free and fat-free, and can also be gluten-free

Serves 8-10

Preparation 20 minutes, cooking 50 minutes for a large cake, 40 minutes for 2 tins and 25-30 minutes for small loaf tins

I first made this cake 20 years ago for my dad who was diabetic and had heart failure. Once a year my brother, sisters and their families and my dad would have a family holiday somewhere in the UK and also abroad. I would make enough bakes and cakes for fourteen people for a week. My dad would be sad because his conditions made it difficult for him to eat the treats. I decided to work on recipes that he could safely eat. This is when I began to develop lower-sugar recipes. At first I called this cake 'Sanctimonious Cake' because you felt righteously good when you'd eaten it. I later gave the recipe to my brother to use in Croot's Farm Shop and Kitchen. I developed the recipe with Margaret, his chief baker at the time, and it won a Great Taste award.

INGREDIENTS

250g stoned dried dates roughly chopped

300ml water

170g wholemeal self-raising flour (or gluten-free self-raising flour)

1 level teaspoon baking powder

1 teaspoon mixed spice

¼ teaspoon cinnamon

500g dried fruit (250g chopped dried apricots, 150g sultanas and 100g raisins or you can use cherries or dried cranberries)

50g ground almonds

zest of two oranges

80ml freshly squeezed orange juice

METHOD

1. Set the oven to 160°C fan, 180°C, 350°F, gas 4-5.
2. Line a 2lb loaf tin or two 1lb loaf tins, or four half-pound loaf tins, or a 23cm deep loose-bottomed round tin.
3. Put the dates and water in a microwaveable bowl and cook for 10 minutes on medium power; the water should be just bubbling. Or you can simmer the dates over low heat in a pan for 10 minutes. Then set aside.
4. Sieve the flour, baking powder and spices into a bowl and add to the date mixture.
5. Add the almonds, zest and orange juice.
6. Mix well until all the flour is incorporated.
7. Spoon into the loaf tin/tins.
8. Bake for 45-50 mins or until a skewer comes out clean.
9. Turn out onto a cooling rack and allow to cool.

Store in an airtight container. This cake keeps really well for up to a week or more; the fruits mature and give the cake moisture that doesn't dry out. Can be frozen for up to a month.

The cake doesn't rise much, in fact it stays pretty flat (which is perfect for a celebration cake) so I slightly mound up the middle of the cake so it looks like it has risen. I have made this twice for wedding cakes and it has been praised for its flavours.

Courgette (zucchini), lime & pistachio cake

Courgettes add moisture to a cake in the same way as carrots do, and the limes give the cake a real summer flavour.

INGREDIENTS

3 medium eggs

125ml rapeseed or sunflower oil

150g caster sugar

225g self-raising flour

½ teaspoon bicarbonate of soda

½ teaspoon baking powder

1 level teaspoon ground cinnamon

250g courgette, finely grated and squeezed out to remove some of the moisture

zest of ½ an unwaxed lime

For the icing

400g cream cheese

200g icing sugar

zest of a lime

2 tablespoons lime juice

40g pistachio nuts, finely chopped

For the lime curd filling and topping

4 large free-range eggs

zest and juice of 5 large juicy unwaxed limes

350g golden caster sugar

225g unsalted butter, cut into small cubes

1 level tablespoon cornflour

Makes 12 small or 8 larger portions
Preparation 20 minutes, baking 30-40 minutes, lime curd 25 minutes

METHOD

1. Preheat the oven to 160°C fan, 180-190°C, 350-375°F, gas 4-5.
2. Line and grease two 23cm-diameter spring-release baking tins or sandwich tins, or a 30cm x 23cm shallow tin or 2 brownie pans.
3. Beat together the eggs, oil and sugar in a large bowl until creamy.
4. Sift the flour, bicarbonate of soda, baking powder and cinnamon, then add to the egg mixture and beat well with an electric or hand-held mixer, or by hand.
5. Stir in the grated courgettes and lime zest until well combined. Divide the mixture into the cake tins.
6. Bake in the middle of the oven for 25–30 minutes. The cake is ready when it is firm to touch and springs back.
7. Remove from the oven and leave for two minutes, then turn out onto a wire rack. Carefully peel off the paper lining and leave to cool.

At this stage you can freeze the cakes in a container for up to a month, placing parchment between each cake.

For the icing

8. Beat the cream cheese in a bowl until smooth. Sift in the icing sugar and stir in the lime juice.
9. Spread two thirds of the icing on the top of one cake (if you've used the shallow baking tin, cut the cake in half horizontally and spread icing on one half only). Then spread about 3 tablespoons of lime curd filling on top of the cream cheese icing. Sandwich the two cakes together.
10. Use the remaining icing to cover the top of the cake, allowing it to drizzle over the edge a little.
11. Sprinkle with the chopped pistachio nuts and lime zest.
12. Using an icing bag, drizzle 2 tablespoons of lime curd over the top of the cake in a zig zag pattern.

This cake will keep for six days. You can freeze it without the icing and then ice it when required after thawing first.

For the lime curd filling and topping

13. Preheat the oven to 150°C fan, 160°C, 325°F, gas 3.
14. Place four jam jars in the oven to sterilise them.
15. Lightly whisk the eggs in a saucepan (or the top pan of a double boiler), add the rest of the ingredients and place the pan over a medium heat (if using the double boiler, half-fill the bottom pan with boiling water, then place the top pan on top, making sure the water doesn't touch it).
16. Whisk continuously using a balloon whisk until the mixture thickens - about 7-8 minutes.
17. Lower the heat to a minimum and let the curd gently simmer for a further minute, continuing to whisk.
18. You can test whether the curd is set by coating the back of a wooden spoon and running your finger through the coating. Your finger should leave a trail that does not close up. This is a good opportunity to taste the curd! If it is not ready, continue on the lowest heat, whisking for another minute or more.
19. Remove the pan from the heat and pour the lime curd into the hot sterilised jars, filling them as full as possible.
20. Cover straightaway with waxed discs, seal while still hot and label when cold.

Store the cold jars in the fridge as this helps keep the curd for several weeks.

I suggest using plain yoghurt but the recipe also works well with a flavoured yoghurt, especially if you want to add some soft fruit of the same flavour.

Chocolate, yoghurt & raspberry cake

Serves 8

Preparation 20 minutes, cooking 50-60 minutes

It's a family joke that after the evening meal when the children would ask for pudding, I would say, 'there's plenty of yoghurts in the fridge'. They remind me of this when they visit today with the grandchildren, because I'm still saying it!

INGREDIENTS

- 200g full-fat plain yoghurt (I like to use Greek yoghurt)
- 150g sunflower oil
- 250g caster sugar
- 3 eggs
- 1 teaspoon vanilla
- 260g self-raising flour
- 50g cocoa
- ½ teaspoon baking powder
- a pinch of salt
- a pinch of ground cinnamon or nutmeg
- 150g raspberries

METHOD

1. Set the oven to 160°C fan, 180-190°C, 350-375°F, gas 4-5.
2. Grease and line a 23cm springform round baking tin or a 2lb loaf tin.
3. Whisk the yoghurt, oil, sugar, eggs, and vanilla, by hand or with an electric or stand mixer.
4. Sift the flour, baking powder, salt and spice into the liquids and stir just until no lumps remain.
5. Mix in 100g of raspberries and pour the batter into the cake tin.
6. Scatter the remaining 50 raspberries on top of the batter, then bake for 50-60 minutes. Check the cake after 40 minutes and if it is browning too quickly, cover with foil.
7. Listen to the cake after 50 minutes; it will be almost baked and all you should hear is a slight bubbling of the mixture. Bake a little longer if too noisy. When a skewer comes out clean, transfer the cake to a cooling rack and let it cool for 10 minutes before removing it from the tin.

When cool, place in an airtight container. The cake keeps very well for several days in the fridge, or you can freeze it for up to one month.

Variation

Pistachio, yoghurt and cardamom cake

Instead of the raspberries, add 150g unsalted pistachio nuts chopped roughly in a food processor.

Instead of the cinnamon and nutmeg add ½ teaspoon ground cardamom.

Raspberry & fresh cream Victoria sponge

I use a spirit level to check the level of my cakes as I build them up. If it's a cream cake you can add a little extra cream under the cake side that needs levelling up.

You can replace the raspberries and raspberry jam with other fruit and matching jams, to make all sorts of different cakes.

INGREDIENTS

For the sponge

All the ingredients should be at room temperature

300g eggs (weighed out of shells, this is usually 5-6 eggs)

300g caster sugar

300g soft margarine

300g self-raising flour

12g baking powder

1 teaspoon vanilla extract

1 tablespoon whole milk

For the filling

1 quantity Chantilly cream (see page 14)

100g fresh raspberries (keep 12 aside for decorating)

4 tablespoons good raspberry jam

a few tiny mint leaves

a sprinkle of freeze-dried raspberry powder (optional)

To serve

a little icing sugar to sift over the raspberries

Serves 8-12

Preparation 10 minutes, cooking 35-38 minutes, assembly 12 minutes

For me a Victoria sponge is almost a weekly bake for family and friends. It is so versatile that the addition of a few ingredients transforms it into a huge variety of delicious cakes or into a showstopper.

METHOD

1. Set the oven to 160°C fan, 180-190°C, 350-375°F, gas 4-5.
2. Grease and line two 23cm baking tins.
3. Weigh the eggs into a bowl and add the same weight of sugar and margarine.
4. Sift the flour and baking powder into the bowl.
5. Add the milk and the vanilla extract.
6. Begin to beat the mixture gently. If you are using a stand mixer or hand mixer gently pulse for about 4-5 pulses. This will prevent the flour rising up in clouds and covering both you and your surroundings. Beat faster for 1 minute, and then allow the mixture to stand (this allows the caster sugar to dissolve into the mixture, which gives the cake a softer texture when baked).
7. Continue to beat the mixture for 2 more minutes; it's important not to overbeat as this will knock out the precious air that makes a good light sponge. Pour into the two cake tins.
8. Place the baking tins on the middle shelf and bake for 35-38 minutes; the cakes are baked when they are evenly and lightly golden, and if you listen to them they only whisper a crackle.
9. Remove the tins from the oven and place on a cooling rack. With a sharp knife and in one continuous movement, loosen the cakes from their tins and leave for 2 minutes to cool.
10. Place a parchment or silicone round on top of the cake and tip onto a cooling rack (this prevents the cake getting marked by the cooling rack). Flip the cake back onto another cooling rack and allow to cool completely.

To fill the cake

11. Make sure you have the Chantilly cream ready (see page 14)
12. Place one of the cakes on a cake plate or board, having first placed a little cream on the base to anchor the cake.
13. Using a spatula, spread half the cream onto the cake, leaving it slightly dipped towards the centre of the cake (this is to hold the jam filling).
14. In a bowl, mash the the raspberries (retaining 12 to decorate) and add 4 tablespoons of raspberry jam, stir well, then place spoonfuls of the jam mixture on the cream.
15. Place the second cake on top of the first and press down lightly.
16. Using a spatula, spread a thin layer of cream evenly on the top of the cake.
17. Place the remaining cream in a piping bag fitted with a 6 point star nozzle/tip and pipe 12 swirls evenly around the cake, adding a raspberry in between each swirl. Place a mint leaf next to each raspberry.
18. To serve, sift a little icing sugar over the raspberries, followed by a little of the raspberry powder if you want.

INGREDIENTS

100g soya flour

100g wholemeal flour

100g rolled oats

100g golden linseed (blitz in a blender or a food processor to break up the seeds a little)

50g sunflower seeds

50g pumpkin seeds

50g sesame seeds

50g ground almonds (optional)

300g dried fruit

2 tablespoons sugar alternative (optional – the fruit provides natural sweetness)

½ teaspoon freshly ground nutmeg

1 teaspoon ground ginger

½ teaspoon ground cinnamon

3 level teaspoons gluten-free baking powder

1 tablespoon malt extract

425ml unsweetened soya milk

50g-100g finely chopped stem ginger

zest and juice of an unwaxed orange

Ladies' cake

Serves 8-10
Preparation 15 minutes, fruits and seeds soaking 30 minutes, cooking 90 minutes

You may be wondering what a 'Ladies' cake' is; it simply refers to when I became menopausal and started researching natural remedies to reduce the symptoms. I learned that soya could supply phyto-oestrogens, which could be used in oestrogen replacement therapy. So I developed a healthy cake recipe to suit my own tastes, including soya. I made it for my dad, too, as he had a heart condition and diabetes, so the lack of eggs, fat and sugar were perfect for him. My dad called it 'bird seed cake', I would make him smile by saying 'it won't harm you dad, your feathers will all be fluffed up and you will whistle better than Billy' (Billy was my dad's budgie). Dad ate the cake for breakfast with a tiny spread of butter, he never grew feathers but he had a lovely singing voice.

METHOD

1. Set the oven to 160°C fan, 180-190°C, 350-375°F, gas 4-5.
2. Line and grease a loaf tin.
3. Place all the dried ingredients in a large bowl.
4. Whisk the malt extract into the soya milk, then stir the soya milk mixture, stem ginger, zest and orange juice into the dry ingredients, mix well until all combined and leave to soak for 30 minutes.
5. Spoon the mixture into the loaf tin, and even the surface with a spatula. Make sure any large exposed pieces of fruit are covered with cake mixture.
6. Bake on the middle shelf, checking after 80 minutes; the cake is cooked when a skewer comes out of the cake cleanly. It may take up to 90 minutes or even longer.
7. Remove the cake from the oven and leave to stand for 5 minutes, then turn out onto a cooling rack.

When cool store in an airtight tin; it keeps well in the fridge for up to two weeks, or for two months if frozen.

This cake is best cut in thin slices. It can be eaten on its own or spread with a little soya spread; I used to have a slice each morning as part of my breakfast (accompanied by a soya yoghurt and fresh fruit).

Banana pecan loaf

Serves 8-10
Preparation 15 minutes, cooking 55 minutes

When bananas begin to turn brown and speckled, it's the perfect time to make this cake or loaf. They are sweet and ripe and easy to mash, giving a moist rich banana taste. Add nuts for taste and texture, or extra sultanas. You can use butter instead of margarine but make sure it is soft, not straight from the fridge.

INGREDIENTS

225g self-raising flour

a pinch of fine sea salt

1 rounded teaspoon ground mixed spice

¼ teaspoon cinnamon

75g soft margarine

112g soft brown sugar

2 eggs lightly beaten

½ teaspoon vanilla extract

3 medium bananas peeled and mashed plus one to split in half

175-200g sultanas

50g pecans or walnuts broken into small pieces

1 tablespoon Demerara sugar

METHOD

1 Set the oven 160°C, 180-190°C, 350-375°F, gas 4-5.

2 Line and grease a round deep 23cm baking tin, or a 2lb loaf tin.

3 Sift the flour, salt and spices into a bowl.

4 In a separate medium bowl, place the margarine (or butter) and sugar; cream until light and fluffy.

5 Beat the eggs in a separate bowl and add them a little at a time, beating in between each addition. If the mixture curdles (separates slightly), add a little flour and continue to beat.

6 Stir in the mashed bananas, sultanas, vanilla extract and nuts. If the mixture still looks curdled don't worry, the final texture of the cake won't be spoiled.

7 Fold in the flour, salt and spices.

8 Turn into the baking tin, level off with a spatula and make a small hollow in the middle to allow for a rise.

9 Scatter the Demerara sugar evenly over the top of the cake to give a slightly glazed crunchy topping.

10 Cut a banana lengthwise and place half of it on top of the cake.

11 Bake on the middle shelf for 55-70 minutes.

12 Check for readiness after 45 minutes by pushing a skewer into the middle of the cake; it should come out clean. There may be mashed banana in the part of the cake that you are testing, but you will see if this is just moisture from the bananas or uncooked cake mix.

13 Remove from the oven when baked and allow to cool for about 5 minutes in the tin before turning out and placing on a cooling rack.

When cold, seal in an airtight container where it will keep for a week. To freeze, place in freezer bag and label; it will keep for up to three months.

If you are batch baking you can make up to 3 times the recipe in one large bowl at a time. Sometimes, if I'm making the cake for a special occasion, I will use half butter and half soft margarine.

Sticky

This cake tastes better for keeping a day or two, so aim to make it in advance if you can. It freezes well too and when it defrosts it has a lovely sticky top.

This cake might sound too noisy to get out of the oven, because it has a lot of liquid bubbling away, but that's ok because it will continue to cook when out of the oven.

ginger cake with lemon icing

Serves 8-12
Preparation 15 minutes, cooking 50-60 minutes

My family loves anything with ginger in it so this cake is a favourite. I got the recipe over forty years ago and it was called Dutch Honey Cake, but I've added and taken away ingredients over time, so it's now just right for me. I hope you will like it too.

INGREDIENTS

240g self-raising flour

8g bicarbonate of soda

20g ground ginger (reduce this to 10g if you don't want too much heat in the cake)

4g ground cinnamon

5g mixed spice

120g butter, cut into small cubes, plus extra for greasing

115g dark muscovado sugar

100g black treacle

100g golden syrup

30g runny honey

250ml whole milk

100g stem ginger, finely chopped

1 egg, lightly beaten

For the icing

50g icing sugar, sifted

1 teaspoon finely grated lemon zest

1 tablespoon lemon juice

1 teaspoon ginger syrup from the stem ginger jar

METHOD

1. Set the oven to 160°C fan, 180-190°C, 350-375°F, gas 4-5.
2. Grease and line an 18cm-diameter 7cm-deep baking tin or a 2lb loaf tin.
3. Sift the flour, bicarbonate of soda and the spices into a large mixing bowl. Add the butter and rub in with your fingertips until the butter has disappeared and the mixture looks like fine breadcrumbs.
4. Put the sugar, treacle, golden syrup, honey and milk into a pan and heat gently until the sugar has dissolved. Once the sugar has dissolved, allow the mixture to come up to boiling point.
5. Stir the stem ginger into the flour mixture, then add the golden syrup mixture, stirring with a wooden spoon until the flour is fully combined.
6. Stir in the egg until completely combined. Don't worry if it seems thinner than most cake mixtures.
7. Pour the mixture into the prepared tin and bake for 50-60 minutes.
8. Check to see if baked after 50 minutes. It's not done if you can hear a furious crackle; you must wait for a slight chatter. The skewer test will give you a good guide as to whether it is baked. Push the skewer at an angle into the centre of the cake and leave for about 3 seconds; it should come out fairly clean.
9. Leave in the tin for 5 minutes before turning out onto a cooling rack.
10. If you are making the cake for the next day, make the icing. If you are freezing it, leave out the icing at this stage.

To make the icing

11. Place the icing sugar in a bowl, add the lemon zest, lemon juice and ginger syrup. Stir until combined and smooth.
12. Only add the icing once the cake has cooled; drizzle it over the cake informally, and allow it to drizzle down the sides.

Store in an airtight container; it will mature nicely in about two days (if you manage not to eat it!). It also freezes well – thaw it before icing it.

Cinnamon rock cakes

Makes 20 large rock cakes or 40 smaller ones
Preparation 15 minutes, cooking 15-20 minutes

My friend Hazel gave me her original recipe and over the years I have changed the ingredients to suit the tastes of my family and friends. I have added a little cinnamon and mixed spice for warmth, and vanilla because it goes well with cinnamon. Hazel is a school/college cook and, like me, she bakes in large batches, so this recipe is designed for a batch bake. For a family-sized bake, divide the recipe by four; 'easy peasy lemon squeezy' is what my children in school would say.

INGREDIENTS

1kg self-raising flour

500g caster sugar

1g baking powder

½ teaspoon ground cinnamon

½ teaspoon ground mixed spice

25g milk powder

250g margarine, cubed

250g unsalted butter, cubed

250g dried fruit (I like to use 150g sultanas and 100g currents)

4 medium eggs, lightly beaten

150ml water

1 teaspoon of vanilla extract

a little extra sugar for sprinkles (optional)

METHOD

1. Set the oven to 170°C fan, 200°C, 400°F, gas 6.
2. Mix the flour, sugar, baking powder, spices and milk powder in a bowl and rub in the cubed margarine and butter until the mixture looks like breadcrumbs, then mix in the dried fruit.
3. In another bowl, beat the egg and water together with the vanilla extract.
4. Add the egg mixture gradually to the dry ingredients (add it a teaspoon at a time in order to make the mixture stick together). Stir with a spoon until the mixture just comes together as a thick, lumpy dough. Don't pour all the egg mixture in at once as flour absorbs liquid at different rates.
5. If you are making giant rock cakes, place tennis-ball-sized spoons of the mixture onto a prepared baking tray. Leave space between them as they will flatten and spread out to double their size during baking.
6. If you are making smaller rock cakes, place golf-ball-sized spoons of mixture, again leaving plenty of space between them .
7. Bake for 15-20 minutes, until golden-brown. Sprinkle with a little caster sugar or Demerara sugar (for a crunchy rock cake) or leave plain.
8. Allow to cool for a couple of minutes, then turn them out onto a wire rack to cool further.

These keep well in an airtight container for three days, or you can freeze them for up to a month.

You could use dried cranberries, dried cherries, glacé cherries or Bing cherries instead of sultanas.

Coconut tarts

INGREDIENTS

For the sweet shortcrust pastry

150g unsalted butter

250g plain flour plus a little extra for rolling out

50g icing sugar

a pinch of salt

2 egg yolks (18g)

30ml ice cold water

For the filling

50g soft margarine

50g caster sugar

1 egg, beaten

1 teaspoon coconut extract (optional)

50g desiccated coconut

10g self-raising flour (optional)

quarter of a jar of raspberry jam

Serves 12

Preparation for the pastry 15 minutes + 1 hour chilling, for filling and assembling 20 minutes, cooking 15-20 minutes

I first watched these being made by my mum when I was about five years old; by the time I was twelve I was making them each week and from then on there was no stopping me. I usually double the recipe and make twenty-four tarts, twelve to keep out and twelve to freeze (I defrost them overnight so they are ready for the next day). If you are short of time you can buy ready-made sweet shortcrust pastry.

METHOD

To make the pastry

1. Rub the fat into the flour, icing sugar and salt until the mixture resembles breadcrumbs.
2. Make a well in the middle of the mixture and pour in the egg yolk and a little of the water, sufficient to bind the pastry into a firm dough. Flours vary and you may need all of the water.
3. Turn onto a lightly floured board and knead lightly (I find about 20-30 turns of the pastry will get it nice and smooth).
4. Roll the pastry into a flattish round the size of a tea plate, wrap in clingfilm and chill for an hour if you have time, or minimum 15 minutes.

To make the filling

5. Cream the fat and the sugar until pale and fluffy.
6. Add the beaten egg a little at a time. If the mixture curdles (separates slightly), don't worry, add a teaspoon of flour and when you add the other ingredients it will be fine.
7. With a metal spoon, fold in the coconut extract, desiccated coconut and flour. You can leave the flour out here and it will give you a softer filling. The mixture should be a good dropping consistency; if it isn't then add a dessert spoon of water.

To assemble

8. Set the oven to 190°C fan, 230°C, 450°F, gas 7-8.
9. Grease a 12-hole tart or patty tin.
10. Remove the pastry from the fridge; allow it to come to room temperature for about 5 minutes.
11. Lightly flour a work surface and roll out the pastry to the thickness of a pound coin (or a Euro, or a dollar).
12. Using an 8cm fluted cutter, cut out 12 rounds and gently press them into the prepared tart/patty tin.
13. Into each tart put a half teaspoon of jam.
14. Dip a dessert spoon into hot water and use it to put a spoonful of the coconut mixture in each tart. Dip the spoon in hot water between each spoonful, to get a nicely rounded top for each tart.
15. Bake the tarts in the oven for 15-20 minutes until golden and firm to touch.
16. Lift out and cool on a wire rack.

When cold these tarts can be stored for up to two weeks or frozen for six weeks.

INGREDIENTS

200g eggs

200g caster sugar

200g soft margarine

150g self-raising flour

50g cocoa powder

6g baking powder

a pinch of salt

2 teaspoons vanilla extract

1 dessertspoon Christmas red colour paste (do not use liquid colour as this won't give the depth of colour)

For the rose buttercream icing

600g icing sugar

200g unsalted butter

50g cream cheese

2 tablespoons rose syrup or rose water

a few drops of pink food gel

For the cupcake filling

3 tablespoons rose petal jelly

To decorate

gold food spray and other toppings (optional)

Try this with Chantilly cream (see page 14) to make a less rich filling.

Red velvet rose cupcakes

Makes 24 (or a 3-tier round cake)
Preparation: cake 15 minutes, filling and buttercream 15 minutes, baking 18-22 minutes, assembly 20 minutes

I love making cupcakes and these are really special, but you can also make a lovely layered cake. There are two important ingredients: rose syrup and rose petal jam, which turn a simple cupcake into a delight.

METHOD

To make the cakes

1. Set the oven to 160°C fan, 180-190°C, 350-375°F, gas 4-5.
2. Grease and line one or two 12-hole muffin baking tins, or 3 x 23cm-diameter loose-bottomed sponge tins.
3. Place the eggs, sugar and margarine in a mixing bowl or stand mixer bowl, sift in the flour, cocoa powder, baking powder, salt and run on a low speed (or beat by hand) until fully combined.
4. Add the vanilla extract and food colouring and mix on low speed (or hand-beat) to spread the colour through the mixture. Turn the mixer to almost full speed and beat for 2 minutes.
5. In each muffin case place 40-42g of mixture, or split the mixture between the 3 baking tins.
6. Bake for about 20 minutes (25 minutes for the larger round cakes). Check after 18 minutes; the muffins should look slightly rounded and firm and if you listen to them they will only make the odd sizzle.
7. Place on a cooling rack to cool.

To make the buttercream filling

8. Place the butter and the cream cheese in a bowl and beat on medium speed (or by hand) to combine the two.
9. Continue to beat on medium as you add the icing sugar a dessert spoon at a time. Stop occasionally and use a plastic scraper to scrape the buttercream from the sides of the bowl.
10. When the icing sugar is almost used up, switch off and add the rose syrup or rose water and pink colour, then beat until fully combined. Add the rest of the icing sugar as before and beat for another 6 minutes. You should have a pink buttercream that is light, fluffy and stands in peaks. If you need, add a little more colour or icing sugar.
11. Place a third of the buttercream in another bowl and stir in the 3 tablespoons of rose-petal jam.
12. With a sharp serrated knife held at an angle, cut around the top of each cupcake to hollow out the middle.
13. In each hollow, place a dessert spoon of the rose-petal-jam buttercream and gently press the 'lid' back on. Don't worry if a little of the buttercream is showing, you will cover it with the piped topping.
14. To finish, fit a piping nozzle onto a piping bag and stand the bag in a jug while you half fill it with buttercream.
15. Hold the piping bag vertically about a centimetre above a cupcake. Steadily squeeze the piping bag while moving the nozzle from the centre to the edge of the cupcake, then make a whorl of icing from the outer edge back to the centre. Stop squeezing the piping bag and lift the nozzle away from the cupcake.
16. Repeat with each cupcake, refilling the piping bag if necessary. Add a topping of your choice to each one. Maybe add some gold spray to give the cupcakes that extra bling.

REDROW
BAKE

Easter cupcakes

Makes 12-16

Preparation 15 minutes, baking 15-20 minutes, decorating 20-30 minutes

'Easy peasy', I only use one method for these and this is it. This is a good recipe for batch baking and it can be used for other celebrations besides Easter, such as Christmas, summer picnics and birthdays. These are chocolate; at other times you might make plain ones and add a different flavour, lemon, orange, coffee or whatever takes your fancy.

INGREDIENTS

170g soft margarine

170g caster sugar

140g self-raising flour

30g cocoa powder

4g baking powder

170g eggs (weighed out of shells; probably 3-4 eggs)

1 tablespoon whole milk

1 teaspoon vanilla extract (or flavouring of your choice)

3 teaspoons chocolate extract

For the buttercream

See recipe on page 14

To decorate

assorted toppings of your choice

METHOD

1. Set the oven to 160°C fan, 180°C, 350-375°F, gas 4-5.
2. Place cupcake cases in a 12-hole baking tray.
3. Put all the cupcake ingredients into a bowl and beat for two minutes.
4. To make sure every cupcake is perfect, place the baking tray on your scales and set them to zero. Into each cupcake case, spoon exactly 40 grams of mixture, zeroing your scales between each one. If this feels too time-consuming, use a dessert spoon of mixture in each case.
5. Bake in the oven for 18 minutes before checking to see if they are cooked. Cupcakes love to be listened to – they have so much to say! They should be done after 20 minutes and when you listen to them they will make the odd crackle.
6. Place on a cooling rack and while they're cooling, make the buttercream.
7. Spread the buttercream on with a knife or pipe it on before adding any other toppings appropriate to the occasion.

These cakes will freeze, and can be kept for up to three weeks. They are best taken out of the freezer and thawed for 3 hours before serving.

Variation

You can make this into a round Easter celebration cake by dividing the mixture between two 23cm round cake tins. Then you can use the buttercream to sandwich them together and as a topping.

INGREDIENTS

170g eggs (weighed out of their shells; probably 3-4 eggs), lightly beaten

170g caster sugar

170g soft margarine

170g self-raising flour

4g baking powder

1 tablespoon whole milk

1 teaspoon lemon extract

zest of 1 unwaxed lemon

For the filling and Chantilly cream

1 quantity Chantilly cream (see page 14)

1 quantity home-made lemon curd (see page 126)

or 1 jar of good quality lemon curd

1 teaspoon lemon extract

3 tablespoons Elderflower liqueur or cordial

zest of two unwaxed lemons (optional)

Elderflower & lemon cupcakes

Makes 12-18

Preparation 15 minutes, cooking 18-20 minutes, decorating 15 minutes

For me as a child, the scent of early summer was always elderflower, red current and privet blossom. Elderflower as a drink and a flavour for cakes has become very popular, and teaming it with sharp tangy lemon curd makes a winning combination.

METHOD

1. Set the oven 160°C fan, 180-190°C, 350-375°F, gas 4-5.
2. Place muffin cases in each hole of a twelve-hole baking tray.
3. Weigh the eggs into a bowl and then add the same weight of all the other ingredients, and beat them for one minute. Allow to rest for one minute before beating for two more minutes. Pour into muffin cases and bake in the oven for 18 minutes before checking. Cupcakes love to be listened to! If they are too noisy put them back in the oven for another two minutes.
4. Place on a cooling rack to cool completely.

To assemble the cupcakes

5. With a sharp knife cut a small round cavity out of the top of each cupcake and set aside.
6. Place a small amount of lemon curd in each cavity, and gently replace the tops, pressing down slightly. Don't worry if a little curd slips out of the edges; it will be covered by the cream.
7. Take a piping bag with a 6-point nozzle and half-fill with the Chantilly cream.
8. Holding the bag vertically about 3cm above a cupcake, pipe on a swirl, and repeat for each cupcake.
9. In a separate piping bag place a little lemon curd, and drizzle over the top of each cupcake.
10. Lastly, add a little lemon zest to each one.

Try adding blackberries or ripe chopped fresh apricots or peaches. Combining fruits is also delicious, such as peach and raspberry; or you might add a little ground cinnamon or ground cardamom.

Raspberry heart friands

Makes 12
Preparation 20 minutes, baking 20-25 minutes

I love making sponges and this is a particularly good one, it's flavoured with almonds and given an extra warmth with a little vanilla. My family and friends love these, they are soft and delicious and full of fresh fruity flavour. I treated myself to some heart-shaped friand pans and I have also got some friand finger pans and some madeleine pans (I love collecting baking pans). You might like to treat yourself to some or you can use simple cupcakes pans, well greased with butter.

INGREDIENTS

230g icing sugar plus extra for dusting

60g plain flour

200g ground almonds

zest of an unwaxed lemon

3 large egg whites (save the yolks and make some sweet or savoury pastry)

2 teaspoons almond extract

2 teaspoons vanilla extract

230g unsalted butter, melted and cooled

200g fresh raspberries (or 100g raspberries and 100g fresh blueberries)

METHOD

1. Set the oven to 160°C fan, 180-190°C, 350-375°F, gas 4-5.
2. Grease 12 friand pans or small cupcake tins with butter.
3. In a bowl stir the icing sugar and flour to combine and make sure there are no lumps, then add the ground almonds and lemon zest.
4. Whisk the egg whites until soft peaks form, then add to the almond mixture, and add the extracts and melted butter.
5. Fold the ingredients gently to combine, lastly folding in two-thirds of the soft fruits.
6. Divide the mixture equally into the pans, and top each with 3 or 4 of the remaining berries.
7. Bake in the centre of the preheated oven for 20-25 minutes, checking after 20 minutes; take out of the oven when the centres spring back when touched.
8. Allow the friands to cool for about 4 minutes to firm up, before turning out onto a cooling rack. Hold another rack over the friands and flip the rack over so they are the right side up.
9. When cool, dust with icing sugar and serve.

To store, they can be stacked with scrunched up baking parchment between them, no higher than two layers as these are really tender. They will store in the fridge for three days, and freeze well too but mine never seem to last that long!

You can make 3–4 batches with the same basic mixture and simply change the flavour or add different ingredients, such as berries, fruits, chocolate and sweets.

INGREDIENTS

175g plain flour

20g baking powder

½ teaspoon cinnamon

80g caster sugar

125g unsalted butter, melted

2 eggs lightly beaten

250ml whole milk

1 teaspoon vanilla extract

200g blueberries, blackberries or raspberries

50g Demerara sugar for topping

For Chantilly cream

one quantity of Chantilly cream (see page 14)

Blueberry muffins

Makes 12 muffins
Preparation 15 minutes, cooking 20-25 minutes

This was the first kind of muffin I ever made and it is still a family favourite. I began when my children were teenagers; until then I made 'buns', but as my children grew, making muffins and cupcakes sounded more sophisticated. I went mad and made all kinds of muffins, usually with melted butter or sunflower oil. I have suggested two alternative decoration ideas: one is simply to scatter with Demerara sugar, while for the second, you might try some Chantilly cream and pipe swirls on the top.

METHOD

1. Set the oven to 180°C fan, 220°C, 425°F, gas 7.
2. Place 12 muffin cases in a muffin tin, or butter it.
3. Sieve the flour, baking powder and cinnamon into a large bowl, stir in the sugar and make a well in the middle of the dry ingredients.
4. Place the butter in a microwaveable bowl and set on low heat for 1 minute (or melt in a pan over low heat).
5. In a separate bowl mix the melted butter, eggs, milk and vanilla extract.
6. Pour the egg mixture into the flour mixture and fold until just combined (do not over mix the batter; it will look quite lumpy but don't worry).
7. Fold in the fruits of your choice.
8. Scoop the batter by heaping quarter-cupfuls into the prepared muffin pan; a muffin scoop works well here. Or you can be precise like me and weigh 75g into each muffin case.
9. Sprinkle about 1 teaspoon or less of Demerara sugar on top of each muffin (if you prefer to put cream on the muffins then miss this out).
10. Bake the muffins for about 20 minutes, until they are light golden brown on top and a skewer inserted into the middle of one of the central muffins comes out clean. It's hard to listen to these muffins because they are so full of fruit they continue to sing for ages.
11. Remove the muffins from the oven, leave to cool for 5 minutes and then take out of the baking tin and transfer to a rack to cool.
12. If you are adding Chantilly cream as a topping, fill a piping bag with a Wilton no 2 nozzle/tip, then pipe swirls of Chantilly cream on each muffin, add a berry or other decoration, and serve or place in the fridge until needed.

Muffins should really be eaten fresh but they can be made earlier, boxed up and frozen.

Instead of Chantilly cream you can use chocolate buttercream

Double chocolate chip muffins

Makes 12

Preparation time 15 minutes, cooking time 20-25 minutes

These muffins are for chocoholics, they are perfect Friday treats when all you crave is chocolate to keep you going to the weekend. I make them for sales and they always sell well either individually, in twos or in fours. Any kind of muffin is quick, easy to make and perfect for treats, and this one is very similar to the blueberry muffin one, but with a few different ingredients, which completely alter the flavour and the look of the muffin.

INGREDIENTS

125g plain flour

50g cocoa powder

20g baking powder

125 g unsalted butter, melted

2 eggs lightly beaten

250ml whole milk

2 teaspoons vanilla extract

200g of chocolate chips either milk, plain or white

For Chantilly cream

one quantity of Chantilly cream (see page 14)

2 teaspoons chocolate extract (optional)

To decorate

chocolate Oreo bicuits, chocolate buttons or try a sprinkle of cocoa powder

METHOD

1. Set the oven to 210°C, 180°C fan, 415°F, gas 6-7.
2. Place muffin cases in a muffin tin, or butter the tin.
3. Sieve the flour, baking powder and cocoa powder into a large bowl, mix in the sugar, and make a well in the middle.
4. Melt the butter in a microwave on low setting for 1 minute, or heat in a pan over low heat till melted.
5. Mix together the melted butter, eggs, milk and vanilla extract.
6. Add the egg mixture to the flour mixture and fold until just combined; it may look lumpy but that's alright, you mustn't over mix it.
7. Fold in the chocolate chips.
8. Scoop the batter into the prepared muffin tin, using a muffin scoop or a small cup.
9. Bake for about 20 minutes, until they are light golden brown on top, and a skewer inserted into one of the central muffins comes out clean.
10. Take out of the oven, leave to cool for 5 minutes and then transfer them from the muffin tin to a rack to cool.
11. When the muffins have cooled, you can add a Chantilly cream topping (see page 14), either made with vanilla extract or – even more chocolatey – adding chocolate extract instead. Then you can decorate as you want.

SPELT
FLOUR
HIGH FIBRE
A blend of our wholegrain and white spelt flours, created to make the perfect loaf

Brownies, biscuits & cookies

I love the fact that in Candice Brown's book 'Comfort', her chapter on brownies, biscuits and tray bakes is called 'BBTs'! So for mine I chose 'BBC', brownies, biscuits and cookies. Well, the BBC did choose me for the Great British Bake Off in 2016!

Except for the gingerbreads (which can take time if you decorate them) these recipes are quick and easy to make. There are bakes for different seasons but you can bake them any time of year.

I've put in a lot of brownie recipes, but I do love chocolate in this squidgy form. I learned a tip from James Hillery who was on Bake Off in 2017: you can put the cooled baked brownie pan in the fridge for two hours to retain the 'squidgyness'. Have I invented a new baking technical term?

Paul Hollywood bakes his brownies in a pan placed in a bain-marie (a tray with boiling water added to about half way up the brownie pan).

See the recipe for this outrageous sundae on page 78

Some suggestions for brownie toppings: thin Oreo cookies, chopped up chocolate bars, chocolate sauce or salted caramel drizzled on-let your imagination go wild, I do.

Quick & easy brownies

Makes 12-16
Preparation 15 minutes, cooking 25-30 minutes

I love dark chocolate and when I learned how to make brownies in my early married life I was hooked. The richness of the dark chocolate really was sublime and at that time I didn't know that dark chocolate was full of polyphenols which are good for you. Once again, all things in moderation; cut brownies into small squares and don't feel too guilty – it's a treat.

INGREDIENTS

200g butter

75g dark chocolate (70-75% cocoa)

2 large eggs, beaten

225g granulated sugar

75g self raising flour

2 teaspoons vanilla extract

1 teaspoon chocolate extract

100g chocolate chips or chopped chocolate pieces

METHOD

1. Set the oven to 160°C fan, 180-190°C, 350-375°F, gas 4-5.
2. Grease and line a shallow brownie tin.
3. Cut butter and chocolate into small pieces so that they melt evenly, then microwave on medium heat for 1 minute, remove to stir, repeat this again and it should be mostly melted (only ever microwave chocolate on low to medium and for one minute at a time to prevent it from burning). Or you can use a double boiler, making sure the top pan doesn't touch the water.
4. Beat the mixture until smooth, then fold in the other ingredients, blending gently but thoroughly so that you don't knock the air out of the mixture.
5. Spread the mixture evenly in the tin, adding any extra topping you want.
6. Place on the middle shelf of the oven and bake for 25 minutes. The centre should be very moist and if you gently shake the tin it should wobble slightly; the brownie mixture will continue to set when out of the oven.
7. Remove from the oven and allow to cool in the tin.

The brownies will keep well in an airtight container for about a week.

Variations

You can leave out the chocolate chips and use 125g of toasted pecans or mixed pecans and brazil nuts instead.

Friday outrageous sundaes

To serve 4
Preparation time 10 minutes

On high days and holidays I make a very special pudding. I had it first in TGI Fridays over thirty years ago and still love it as a treat. Time for some name dropping: when I did Comic Relief in the spring of 2017, I was asked to create a pudding suitable for serving in a pizza restaurant and I decided to make 'Friday Outrageous Sundae'. The pudding went down very well and made almost £200 before I ran out of ingredients.

INGREDIENTS

4 brownies – you may use any of the brownie recipes in this book

I litre of good quality vanilla ice cream

200ml double cream

4 tablespoons caramel or chocolate sauce (see the toppings section, pages 16-17)

1 bag of Maltesers

1 bag of Smarties or M&Ms

or 100g chocolate chips

or a little of all three of the above

METHOD

1. Place 4 brownies on a microwaveable dish and heat for 1 minute until warm, or heat in a warm oven for 5 minutes.
2. Roughly chop the brownies and share them out between 4 sundae glasses, then spoon in a scoop or two of good quality ice cream followed by a generous piping of whipped cream; top with maltesers, chocolate chips, a drizzle of salted caramel, or a drizzle of chocolate sauce and serve straightaway.

This used to be a perfect treat for my staff at the end of a hard term when all they craved to keep going was chocolate!

Turkish Delight chocolate brownies

INGREDIENTS

200g dark chocolate

125g unsalted butter

2 medium eggs beaten lightly

100g caster sugar

76ml whole milk

2 teaspoons vanilla extract

1 teaspoon rose water depending on how rose-flavoured you want your brownies to be

175g plain flour

15g baking powder

1 tablespoon cocoa

3 Fry's Turkish Delights chopped into small pieces

⅓ jar of rose-petal jam/ conserve

Keep back some of the Turkish Delight pieces to scatter on the top of each brownie mixture before baking.

Makes 12

Preparation 15 minutes, cooking 20-25 minutes

Time for more name dropping. I was lucky enough to be invited to take part in an episode of Paul Hollywood's series 'A Baker's Life'. Selasi (also from Bake Off) and I set a roulade challenge for Paul and he made a hazelnut and rose-petal buttercream roulade. I had not used rose petal conserve before; it was so delicious it made me think of how I might use it in my recipes.

The rose-petal conserve has a Turkish Delight flavour but even more intense, so I decided to team it with Turkish Delights in a brownie. It also teams perfectly with fresh Chantilly cream plopped on top.

METHOD

To make these brownies, use the basic method for Quick & easy brownies on page 77.

This vegan sweet potato brownie recipe can be suitable for low calorie, gluten-free and sugar-free diets (if you use sugar substitute).

Sweet potato brownies

Makes 12-16
Preparation 20 minutes, cooking 20 minutes

I started using sweet potatoes in baking about ten years ago when I found out that they were low GI and can be used in sweet and savoury dishes. This was the time when my sister and her family moved to New York, and visiting them opened my eyes to a whole new set of ingredients and recipes. Sweet potatoes add a sweetness, lightness and moisture to bakes as well as being good for you.

Over the years I've become more aware of food intolerances and folk preferring different diets, including vegetarian and vegan. I used the internet to find recipes and developed them until they were my own.

INGREDIENTS

250g peanut or almond butter (or a nut-substitute spread)

150g sweet potato puree (you can bake or boil the sweet potatoes)

2 teaspoon vanilla extract

50g self-raising flour (oat, white, or spelt flour work well if you are gluten-intolerant and Dove GF self-raising flour is perfect if you need to go gluten-free)

130g granulated sugar or xylitol

40g cocoa powder

15g baking powder

½ teaspoon cinnamon

4g fine sea salt

60g mini chocolate chips, plus more for the top (optional)

METHOD

1. Set the oven to 160°C fan, 180-190°C, 350-375°F, gas 4-5.
2. Line and grease a brownie pan.
3. Gently heat your nut butter until easily stirable.
4. Whisk the softened nut butter with the sweet potato puree and vanilla extract in a large bowl.
5. In a separate bowl, sift together the flour, sugar, cocoa, baking powder, cinnamon and salt.
6. Pour the dry ingredients into sweet potato mixture and fold in until all combined, then add the chocolate chips.
7. Pour into the prepared pan and smooth out evenly, using an offset spatula dipped in water.
8. Sprinkle with a few extra chocolate chips if liked.
9. Bake in the centre of the oven for 20 minutes.
10. It will look a little underdone, and when you shake the pan the centre of the brownie should wobble but it firms up as it cools.
11. When cooled, if it is still too gooey let it sit in the fridge for a few hours – it will still taste delicious.

Keep in the fridge or freeze; when frozen it will last for a month.

Salted caramel brownies

Makes 9 large pieces or 16 small pieces
Preparation 10 minutes, cooking 30-35 minutes

I've made brownies for a long time but when salted caramel became the rage, I thought I'd add it to my brownie repertoire and it was delicious. The combination of sweet and salt really enhances the flavours. As a treat these are up with the 'naughty but nice' ones!

INGREDIENTS

150g dark chocolate chips (70% cocoa) plus extra for sprinkling if desired

50g chocolate (35%-50% cocoa)

200g unsalted butter

1 quantity salted caramel (see page 16)

or a 397g tin Carnation Caramel

1 teaspoon flaked sea salt

200g caster sugar

4 medium eggs

1 teaspoon vanilla extract

1 teaspoon chocolate extract (optional)

130g plain flour

50g cocoa powder

METHOD

1. Set the oven to 160°C fan, 180-190°C, 350-375°F, gas 4-5.
2. Prepare a deep square brownie pan 20cm x 20cm.
3. Place the chocolate and butter in a microwaveable bowl and melt in the microwave for 3 or 4 one-minute bursts on medium power, stirring at the end of every minute. Alternatively, melt the chocolate and butter in a heat-proof bowl over a pan of simmering water, making sure the water doesn't touch the bottom of the bowl. Set the chocolate mixture aside to cool a little.
4. In a small bowl, mix 175g of the caramel with the sea salt and put aside.
5. Put the rest of the caramel in a large bowl with the sugar, eggs and extracts, and beat well until the sugar has dissolved and the mixture is combined.
6. Stir the chocolate mixture into the egg mixture.
7. Sift the flour and cocoa powder, then fold into the chocolate mixture using a figure of eight motion to keep the mixture light.
8. Place half the mixture in the baking pan and allow it to run to the corners of the pan. Level off with a spatula.
9. Using a teaspoon, spoon half the remaining caramel across the brownie mixture. Spoon the rest of the brownie mixture evenly over the top.
10. Spoon the rest of the caramel (except for a tablespoonful) informally over the brownie and use a skewer to drag the caramel around to create a pattern.
11. Place on the middle shelf of the oven and bake for 25-30 minutes; check after 25 minutes. It is ready when the middle is still slightly soft and wobbly. It will continue to cook for a little once out of the oven.
12. Place the pan on a cooling rack and allow to cool before cutting and storing in an airtight container.
13. Before serving, drizzle with the tablespoon of salted caramel or use a piping bag to pipe it on.

They stay fresh for about three days but can be frozen for two months.

Beetroot brownies

These can be made gluten-free if you exchange the plain flour for gluten-free plain flour.

Makes 12
Preparation 20 minutes, cooking 35-40 minutes

Baking with beetroot is something you will either love or just not get your head around. I love beetroot in savoury recipes and I'm only now experimenting with it as a sweet ingredient. I was given this brownie recipe by Jane who is the recipe developer for Florette. I'm sure she will be pleased that I want to share it.

INGREDIENTS

350g cooked beetroot (reserve 1 tablespoon of the coarse puree for the icing). You can use fresh beetroot, or ready-cooked which saves you getting red hands.

300g dark chocolate (70% cocoa) roughly chopped or chocolate chips

75g unsalted butter

3 eggs

200g granulated sugar

2 teaspoons vanilla extract

4g fine sea salt

50g plain flour

45g cocoa powder

For the icing

100g icing sugar

1 tablespoon of the beetroot puree

METHOD

1 Set the oven to 160°C fan, 180-190°C, 350-375°F, gas 4-5.

2 Grease and line a 23cm x 20cm brownie pan or a similar-size square pan.

3 Drain the beetroot and blitz in the food processor, or medium grate. It's less messy if you use a processor; keep scraping down the sides to make sure no big lumps remain.

4 Melt 200g of the chocolate and butter in a heat-proof bowl over a pan of simmering water (don't let the bowl touch the water), stirring until all is combined and the chocolate is melted.

5 Alternatively you can put the butter and chocolate in a microwaveable bowl and microwave on low for 4 bursts of 1 minute stirring in between.

6 Remove from the heat and set aside.

7 Beat the eggs, sugar, vanilla and salt until all are combined and have a creamy consistency.

8 Beat the egg mixture into the chocolate mixture; stir in the beetroot.

9 Sift the flour and cocoa powder into the chocolate mixture and finally add the remaining chocolate chunks or chips.

10 Pour into the brownie pan and level off with a spatula.

11 Bake for 30-40 minutes until a crust has formed but the middle is still slightly wobbly.

12 Remove from the oven and place on a cooling rack. Allow to cool completely in the tin.

The brownie can be lifted out and kept in the baking parchment. To freeze, use an airtight container (it's fine for up to two months). Get it out of the freezer the day before you need it, to defrost fully before you decorate it with icing.

To make the icing

13 Place the icing sugar and reserved beetroot juice in a bowl and beat. If the mixture is a little thick, loosen it with a few more drops of beetroot juice. Leave to set.

ARL GREY

Spelt & ginger biscuits

Makes approximately 200; divide quantities by 4 to make a perfect home batch
Preparation 1 hour, cooking 7-9 minutes

For many many years I have made ginger biscuits for my family, and we would eat them on trains, boats and planes, even cars. I love Roman history and I once read that the Romans travelled with a bag of ginger to eat to prevent sea sickness. You don't have to be travelling to eat these delightfully spicy warm biscuits, they are an anytime treat and I've been told they are perfect for dunking.

INGREDIENTS

500g unsalted butter

500g golden syrup

500g stem ginger

500g soft light brown sugar

8 egg yolks

2kg spelt white flour

6 teaspoons vanilla extract

16 teaspoons of powdered ginger

½ teaspoon bicarbonate of soda

METHOD

1. Set the oven to 200°C fan, 250°C, 475°F, gas 8-9.
2. Place the butter, golden syrup and stem ginger in a microwaveable bowl and microwave on medium heat until they are just melted, about two bursts of one minute. Or in a medium-sized pan, melt the ingredients over a low heat.
3. Beat in the two sugars, then the egg yolks, flour, ground ginger, bicarbonate and finally the vanilla extract.
4. Stir well until all combined and you have a soft dough.
5. Weigh out small balls of dough – each one should weigh around 20g, which makes a nice little biscuit.
6. Place on the baking tray about 6cm apart.
7. Bake in the oven for 7-9 minutes. They will rise and become golden around the edges; don't let them get too dark as they can taste burnt.
8. Remove them from the oven; they will sink down a little and have a crinkly look about them, let them cool for a moment and use an offset spatula to lift them onto a cooling rack.

Once cool they can be stored in an airtight tin and will keep for up to a month.

Easter biscuits

INGREDIENTS

200g self-raising flour

¼ teaspoon cinnamon

100g caster sugar

100g unsalted butter

rind and juice of half a lemon

1 egg, beaten

For the royal icing

2 egg whites

500g icing sugar

½ teaspoon lemon juice

½ teaspoon glycerine

gel food colouring, lemon, pink and green

Although I decorate these biscuits for Easter, you could decorate them for a different seasonal event or just leave plain and enjoy any time.

Makes 24

Preparation 30 minutes, chilling 15 minutes, cooking 15 minutes

I started making Easter biscuits as a teenager for my family; now I make them with my own two grown-up children and grandchildren. Until I retired, we made them with the school children every year to take home as presents in lovingly-made Easter baskets.

METHOD

1 Set the oven to 160°C fan, 180-190°C, 350-375°F, gas 4-5.

2 Grease and line 3 baking trays.

3 Mix the flour, cinnamon and sugar in a bowl and rub in the butter until the mixture looks like fine breadcrumbs.

4 Add the grated zest, lemon juice and beaten egg, and mix to a stiff paste.

5 Lightly flour a surface and knead the dough for a few turns to make sure the dough is smooth.

6 Roll it out thinly; it should be thinner than a pound coin. I turn the dough once, roll and turn again so that it's evenly rolled out.

7 Use the Easter biscuit-cutters of your choice.

8 Place the biscuits on the baking trays, spacing them 2cm apart.

9 Chill the biscuit dough in the fridge for 15 minutes so the mixture doesn't spread too much.

10 Bake in the oven for about 15 minutes. They are ready when they are lightly golden; the centres should be slightly soft to touch. Do not let them colour too much.

11 Once out of the oven, leave on the baking sheet for 1 minute to become less tender, then lift them carefully onto a cooling rack, using an offset spatula, and leave to cool.

To make the royal icing

12 In a large bowl, whisk the egg whites until frothy. Sift in the icing sugar a tablespoon at a time until the icing is soft but not runny.

13 Stir in the lemon juice and glycerine.

14 Divide the icing into a number of bowls depending on the colours you will be using. Leave one bowl white and then add gel colour to the other bowls, keeping the colours to pastel shades.

15 Put a fine piping nozzle number 3 on an icing bag, then place a small quantity of coloured icing in the bag and squeeze it down towards the nozzle so it fits comfortably in your hand.

16 To ice each biscuit, carefully pipe a little in from the outer edge, following the contours; then continue piping an inner ring. Do this evenly because you are going to spread this icing out.

17 Using a cocktail stick, gently spread the icing until the biscuit is covered. Place the biscuit on a flat surface and shake from side to side to create a super smooth top. Alternatively, pipe different-coloured designs onto the biscuits (see the picture).

18 Leave to set at least 4 hours, or overnight.

19 To finish off the biscuits, add white piping in the design of your choice, and leave to set.

Once the biscuit icing is completely set (this can take overnight) the biscuits can be stored in an airtight container for up to two weeks.

Variation

The traditional Somerset Easter biscuit is round, filled with currants and is flavoured with cassia oil, which gives the biscuits that distinctive Easter biscuit smell and taste. Cassia oil can usually be found in cook shops around Easter.

Add a few drops of cassia oil to the lemon juice. Add 60g currants when the eggs go into the mixture.

Shortbread

Makes 24-30 fingers/biscuits
Preparation 15 minutes, cooking 30-35 minutes

When I make these in a large quantity I use the chilling time to mix up several batches of dough and I double the quantity, making two trays at a time. Sometimes I make shortbread fingers, but it's also fun to make shortbread shapes like the ice cream cones shown in the picture, which are decorated with royal icing (see page 15).

INGREDIENTS

230g plain flour

100g semolina

225g unsalted butter

100g caster sugar

¼ teaspoon vanilla extract

25g Demerara or caster sugar for dusting

METHOD

1. Set the oven to 160°C fan, 180-190°C, 350-375°F, gas 4-5.
2. Grease and line a 30cm x 23cm tray bake tin.
3. Place the flour and semolina in a bowl and combine by hand or with a food processor.
4. Add the butter, sugar and extract and rub in, either with your fingertips or in a processor, until it begins to come together, then knead lightly until the mixture forms a ball.
5. Press the dough into the baking tin, making sure it is level (use an offset spatula to do this). Or roll out on a floured work surface, to about ½ cm thickness, and cut out shapes with biscuit cutters. Then place each biscuit on the tray bake tin.
6. Prick all over with a fork.
7. Chill in the fridge for about an hour or until firm.
8. Place in the oven and bake for 30-35 minutes, checking after 25 minutes. The shortbread should be lightly golden.
9. Take out of the oven and scatter with the caster or Demerara sugar. Leave to cool in the tin for a few minutes and cut into fingers if you haven't already made individual biscuits. Then carefully lift onto a cooling rack, using the offset spatula.
10. Leave to cool completely before packing into an airtight container.

Variations

For Almond shortbread leave out the vanilla extract and add 1 teaspoon almond extract. When you prick the biscuits with a fork, scatter on 50g flaked almonds.

For a Citrus shortbread, add the zest of a lemon or an orange when you add the sugar.

Nut cookies

Makes about 48; to make 12 cookies divide the recipe by 4
Preparation 25 minutes, cooking 15-20 minutes

I used to make these for my children's packed lunches; they are quick to make, and at the time I was working and everything I baked had to be done after the children went to bed. I use Demerara sugar as it produces a crisp crunchy biscuit.

INGREDIENTS

454g unsalted butter

227g Demerara sugar

2 teaspoons vanilla extract

900g plain wholewheat flour (or spelt flour for more substantial cookies)

227g mixed chopped nuts

240ml whole milk

whole nuts for topping

METHOD

1. Set the oven to 180°C fan, 220°C, 425°F, gas 7.
2. Grease and line 4 baking sheets.
3. Cream the butter, sugar and vanilla until well blended.
4. Stir in the flour and add the nuts.
5. Form into rounds about the size of a walnut.
6. If you want them a uniform size, weigh out 20g balls.
7. Place the rounds on the prepared baking sheets and slightly flatten, topping each cookie with nuts, pecans, pistachios or walnuts.
8. Bake for 15-20 minutes until golden brown, leave on the tray to cool for 5 minutes and then place on a cooling rack.

Store in an airtight container until needed, they will keep well for a week.

Variations

Use chocolate chips instead of nuts, or make a batch of half and half.

These cookies are perfect with a cuppa, try resisting dunking them!

Maryland cookies

Makes 50
Preparation 15 minutes, cooking 15-20 minutes

This recipe was given to me by a school cook and I have played with the recipe over the years. The cookies are delightfully crunchy when made with caster sugar but you can use half caster and half soft brown sugar if you want a more chewy cookie.

Make them in batches of 50 or double the ingredients to make 100.

They are good for packed lunches and picnics, they sell well, and they make lovely little gifts!

INGREDIENTS

550g plain flour

14g baking powder

6g bicarbonate of soda

225g caster sugar

225g margarine

115g chocolate chips

250g golden syrup

1 teaspoon vanilla extract

METHOD

1. Set the oven to 170°C fan, 200°C, 400°F, gas 6.
2. Prepare 2 baking sheets.
3. Sieve the flour, baking powder and bicarbonate of soda into a large bowl.
4. Add the sugar and rub in the margarine until the mixture resembles bread crumbs.
5. Add the chocolate chips.
6. Add the syrup and vanilla extract and stir in with a knife. When it begins to come together, knead the mixture by hand.
7. Weigh out 40g of mixture for each cookie, form into a round and place on the baking tins, leaving plenty of space between the biscuits, because they spread. Flatten slightly with a palette knife.
8. Bake for 15-20 minutes until golden.
9. Leave on the baking sheet to firm up for a minute or two before placing on a cooling rack to cool

Once cool pack into an airtight tin; they will keep for several days, and they will also freeze though they are better fresh.

Ginger oat cookies

Makes 12-14

Preparation 15 minutes, cooking 15-20 minutes

I've been making these cookies for years – they are quick and economical to make, they're ideal for cake and bake sales, they make excellent gifts wrapped in pretty packets, and they are my husband's all-time favourite cookie! I tend to double the recipe and do two lots at the same time in separate bowls.

INGREDIENTS

- 172g soft light brown sugar
- 172g soft margarine
- 172g golden syrup
- 200g self-raising flour (or gluten-free self-raising flour)
- ½ teaspoon bicarbonate of soda
- 20g ground ginger (or less if you want less heat)
- a pinch of cinnamon
- 200g rolled oats
- 90g finely chopped stem or crystallised ginger
- 1 teaspoon vanilla extract

METHOD

1. Set the oven to 160°C fan, 180-190°C, 350-375°F, gas 4-5.
2. Grease and line 2 baking sheets.
3. Place the sugar, margarine, and syrup in a pan and allow to melt so that all the ingredients combine. You can also do this in the microwave on medium heat for 2-3 bursts of 1 minute. Allow to cool a little.
4. Sift the flour, bicarbonate of soda and spices into a large bowl and add the oats, stir well and then stir in the ginger pieces.
5. Make a hollow in the middle of the flour mixture, then pour in the melted ingredients, add the vanilla extract and with a wooden spoon stir well until the mixture comes together. Knead into a rough ball.
6. The mixture will be quite soft and will need to cool. Cover the bowl with a clean tea towel, and place in the fridge for 15-20 minutes for the dough to become firm, so that it can be more easily handled.
7. When it feels quite firm, lightly dust your work surface with a little flour, place the dough on the floured area, and with a lightly floured rolling pin roll out to about 1 cm thickness.
8. Cut 12 rounds with cookie cutters and place each cookie on the baking sheet, allowing space between the cookies as they can spread widely.
9. Left-over dough can be rolled out again to make more cookies, it's very forgiving and can be rolled out up to 3 times until used up.
10. Bake in the oven for 15-20 minutes until lightly browned and just firm to touch.
11. Remove from the oven and leave to cool for 4 minutes before transferring to a cooling rack.

When cool, pack in an airtight container or freeze for up to 2 months.

Variations instead of ginger

100-150g chopped soft semi-dried apricots

100-150g chopped glacé cherries plus 2 teaspoons almond extract

100g-150g chocolate chips

50g chocolate chips and 50g chopped nuts

100g mini M&Ms plus a few to sprinkle on top.

100-150g raisins soaked in the zest and juice of an organic unwaxed orange, plus ½ teaspoon ground cinnamon.

Tip

Leave spaces between the cookies as they will spread.

INGREDIENTS

350g plain flour (or gluten-free plain flour or coconut flour) plus extra for rolling

1 teaspoon bicarbonate of soda

1 teaspoon ground ginger

1 teaspoon mixed spice

1 teaspoon cinnamon

¼ teaspoon freshly ground nutmeg

124g butter

175g light soft brown sugar

4 tablespoons golden syrup (weight 100g)

1 free range egg

To decorate

200g icing sugar

water

edible gel colours

edible sprinkles

For royal icing (optional)

see page 15

Festive gingerbread cookies (recipe 1)

Makes 30-40 small biscuits, or fewer if you are making larger items such as gingerbread people
Preparation 20 minutes, cooking 12-14 minutes, plus decorating time

I love making gingerbread cookies and usually use a melting method, but recently I have been baking with very young children (2-4 year olds) and I needed to develop a recipe that does not need to be heated. Also a rubbed-in method is very tactile for little ones, and it can be used straightaway, as tiny folk don't like to wait! The dough does improve if you give it 15 minutes to chill in the refrigerator.

METHOD

1. Set the oven to 170°C fan, 200°C, 400°F, gas 6.
2. Grease and line 2 or 3 baking sheets.
3. Sift the flour, bicarbonate of soda, ginger, mixed spice, cinnamon and nutmeg into a bowl.
4. Cut the butter into small pieces, rub into the flour until it disappears, then stir in the brown sugar.
5. Beat the syrup and egg in a bowl until combined.
6. Stir the syrup mixture into the flour mixture and use a knife to pull it together to make a dough.
7. Place the dough on a lightly floured surface and knead until smooth.
8. Wrap in clingfilm and allow to rest for 15 minutes.
9. Lightly flour the work surface and roll the dough out to the thickness of a pound/dollar coin.
10. Use cookie cutters to cut out shapes and place them on a lined and greased baking tray.
11. Place in the oven and bake for 12 minutes; they are baked when they are slightly risen and golden in colour.
12. Leave on the tray for 1 minute until they have cooled slightly and will be easier to transfer to a cooling rack. If you find that some cookies are touching, use a sharp knife while the cookies are still hot, to cut them apart and tidy the edges.
13. The cookies can be left plain or iced.

To make the icing

14. You can use royal icing (see page 15) or you can use this simple method: place the icing sugar in a bowl and mix with sufficient water to make a stiff spreading or piping consistency.
15. Have fun by adding different colours to your icing, or leave white.
16. A very easy method of icing is to spread icing over a cookie and then dip into sprinkles in shallow wide bowls.
17. Leave overnight or until the icing has set completely. They will keep for at least a month in an airtight container.

Festive gingerbread (recipe 2 – traditional)

I sometimes add 1/2 teaspoon of vanilla extract (at Christmas) or the zest of 1/2 a lemon (at Easter)

Makes 30-40 small biscuits and around 20 if you use large biscuit-cutters
Preparation 20 minutes, cooking 15-20 minutes, plus decorating time

When my children were little I made these delightful buttery gingerbread biscuits, spending hours decorating them while I sang along to carols. When the children came home from school they would help me to finish the biscuits, decorating them with love and personalising them for family members including their grandparents.

INGREDIENTS

1 medium egg

25g molasses (black treacle)

200g caster sugar

2 teaspoons ground cinnamon

2 teaspoon ground cardamom

½ teaspoon freshly ground nutmeg

250g butter

5g baking powder

350g plain flour

For the royal icing

1 quantity of royal icing (see page 15)

1 teaspoon of lemon juice (this flavours the icing and makes it hard)

METHOD

1. Set the oven to 160°C fan, 180-190°C, 350-375°F, gas 4-5.
2. Line and grease a baking tray.
3. Place eggs, treacle, sugar and spices in a bowl and beat well.
4. Melt the butter in a small pan on the hob, or in the microwave on medium for two minutes (or until melted). Let it cool, then stir into the egg mixture.
5. Sift the flour and baking powder and stir into the mixture, binding with a spoon or by hand to make a dough.
6. Wrap the dough in clingfilm or foil and chill in the fridge for 30 minutes; this firms it up and allows the glutens to do their thing.
7. Roll the dough on a lightly floured surface, until it is about 7mm thick (about the thickness of a one pound, dollar or Euro coin).
8. Use a biscuit cutter to cut the shapes you want, then put the biscuits on the baking tray.
9. Bake in the oven for about 15 minutes before checking; they may take up to 20 minutes depending on the thickness of the biscuit. They are done when just firm to touch.
10. Remove from the oven and leave to cool for 5 minutes on the tray before lifting them onto a cooling rack.

The biscuits can be decorated as soon as they are cool.

To decorate

11. Use royal icing (see page 15), and place half the mixture in a piping bag fitted with a plain small-hole nozzle. Pipe onto the biscuits as you choose. Use up the rest of the icing as you need it.

Scones & savouries

Not everyone has a sweet tooth so here are some family favourites. These recipes are good for packed lunches and picnics as well as the supper table, and depending on the size you make them, they are perfect as little appetisers.

Not name-dropping (yes I am), when the 2016 Great British Bake Off final took place with Andrew, Jane and Candice, all the bakers and their families were invited. I took my husband, my brother-in-law and his wife, and two good friends. I also took four dozen sausage rolls, including a dozen vegetarian ones for my lovely fellow baker Rav and his family.

When the last bake was announced, I couldn't believe it: the three finalists were asked to bake a picnic to include sausage rolls – if only I'd still been in the running! But a box of my sausage rolls did find their way to the BBC production team, so I may not have won, but my sausage rolls are famous!

On a more practical note, one thing I've learned over the years is that to bake good scones, biscuits and pastry, you need to get the baking sheet really hot before putting it in to bake.

Fruit scones

Halve the recipe to make a smaller batch; they freeze well so I usually make a big batch and freeze half.

Makes 24
Preparation 15 minutes, baking 14-18 minutes

My first memory of scone-making must have been when I was 3 years old in my Nana's house. She had one of those sturdy dining tables typical of the 1950s with big turned round spindle legs. I would sit under the table and imagine it was my secret place (I now know everyone knew where I was). My Nana would say 'I wonder where Valerie is? I wonder if she wants to help me make scones?' I would come out of my hiding place and kneel on a chair making currant scones with her.

INGREDIENTS

900g strong white bread-flour

50g baking powder

50g custard powder

a pinch of fine sea salt

225g unsalted butter

150g caster sugar

225g sultanas (or a mixture of dried fruits such as currants and sultanas)

zest of an orange (optional)

300ml whole milk

300ml double cream or yoghurt

4 eggs

METHOD

1 Set the oven to 200°C fan, 250C, 425°F, gas 7-8. To rise well, scones need a really hot oven.

2 Grease a baking sheet and heat in the oven while you make the scones.

3 Sieve the flour, baking powder, custard powder and salt into a wide bowl.

4 Cut the butter into small pieces and rub into the flour mixture with your fingertips until it disappears.

5 Stir in the caster sugar, sultanas and orange zest.

6 In a separate bowl beat the milk, cream or yoghurt and eggs until combined and bubbles are appearing.

7 Make a well in the centre of the flour and pour in two-thirds of the egg mixture. Using a knife, combine to make a soft dough; add more liquid as necessary.

8 Knead the dough in the bowl for a few turns to make a ball. On a lightly floured work surface, continue to knead to give a smooth surface, then roll out to about 3 cm thick.

9 Dip the cutter into some flour to prevent it from sticking; cut out scones, re-flouring the cutter as needed, until all the dough is used up.

10 Take the hot baking sheet from the oven and place the scones on it, a little apart. Brush them with remaining egg mixture.

11 Bake for 15-20 minutes; the scones should be well risen, golden, and the bottoms also golden. Break a scone open to see if it is baked. If it's damp, bake for a further 3 minutes.

12 Remove from the oven and place on a cooling rack.

Serve hot, split and spread with butter, or store in an airtight container for up to two days. Reheat in a warm oven to soften them before eating.

Tip: Save a little of the egg mixture to brush the tops of the scones before baking.

Cheese scones

Tip: You can make your own baking powder by combining 1/2 teaspoon of cream of tartar with 1/4 teaspoon of bicarbonate of soda. This provides the equivalent of 1 teaspoon of baking powder, sufficient to use with 110g plain flour.

INGREDIENTS

500g strong bread flour (or whole meal flour or gluten-free flour) plus a little extra for rolling out

50g baking powder

2-4 teaspoons of English mustard powder (you can adjust the quantities of mustard to suit your taste)

¼ teaspoon cayenne pepper

¼ teaspoon fine sea salt

2 teaspoons soft brown sugar

100g unsalted butter at room temperature

100g cheddar cheese, grated

50g Parmesan cheese grated

2 eggs

280 ml plain yoghurt

280 ml whole milk

Makes 24

Preparation 15 minutes, baking 15-20 minutes

My family love these scones, especially my husband (do you say 'sconns' or 'scoanes'?). They are very quick and easy to make, and you can use any hard cheese you like, but living in Somerset I use Cheddar. This recipe uses strong white bread flour so as the scones bake they keep their shape and rise well.

This is a good recipe to double up if you want to make a large batch. You can use wholemeal flour or gluten-free flour; the rise will be less but still tasty.

METHOD

1. Set the oven to 200°C fan, 250°C, 425°F, gas 7-8. The oven needs to be really hot for scones to rise quickly and well.
2. Grease a baking sheet and place in the oven to heat up while you make the scones.
3. Sift the flour, baking powder, mustard, cayenne and salt into a bowl and stir in the brown sugar.
4. Cut the butter into small pieces and toss into the flour mixture.
5. With your fingertips rub in the butter until it disappears.
6. Combine the cheeses. Add the cheese to the flour mixture but keep back about 40g to top the scones.
7. In a separate bowl beat the 2 eggs, add the yoghurt and milk and beat until combined.
8. Make a well in the middle of the flour mixture and pour two-thirds of the egg mixture into the well, using a knife to combine the flour and liquid to make a soft dough. Add more liquid as necessary.
9. Knead the dough by hand in the bowl for a few turns to make a ball.
10. Lightly flour your work surface, place the dough on it and and knead for a further few turns to give a smooth surface.
11. Roll out to about 3 cm thick (half an inch).
12. Dip your scone cutter into a little flour to prevent it from sticking to the dough.
13. Cut out circles of dough, making sure you press the cutter straight down to ensure an evenly cut scone. You may need to re-flour the cutter.
14. Re-form the dough to cut more scones; if you have a small amount of dough left, turn it into a ball and make it your 'taster scone'.
15. Remove the hot baking sheet from the oven and place the scones on the sheet a little apart. Quickly place a little cheese on each scone and put the tray back in the oven.
16. Bake for 15-20 minutes; the scones should be well risen, golden, and the bottoms also golden.
17. I always break a scone open to see if the dough is baked and not damp. If at all damp, I let the scones bake for a further 3 minutes.
18. Remove the scones from the oven and place on a cooling rack.

They are delicious served hot, split and spread with butter, or can be stored cool in an airtight container for up to two days (reheat in a warm oven to soften them before eating).

I often freeze a batch of scones for unexpected visitors.

Variation

Add 1 tablespoon of finely chopped chives.

Cheese & onion pasties

INGREDIENTS

For the pastry

1 medium egg

45ml ice cold water

300g plain flour plus extra for rolling out

150g slightly softened butter, cut into small cubes

4g fine sea salt

a pinch of sugar

For the filling

300g Maris Piper (or other floury) potatoes, peeled, cut into 1 cm cubes

2 tablespoons rapeseed oil

1 large onion, finely chopped

1 large clove garlic, finely minced

200g strong cheddar cheese

100g Parmigiano Reggiano cheese

1 level teaspoon dried mustard powder

a pinch or two of cayenne pepper

2 teaspoons fresh thyme, chopped

2 teaspoons flat-leaf parsley, chopped

3 tablespoons double cream

salt and pepper to taste

For the egg wash

1 egg yolk

3 teaspoons water

a few grains of salt

Makes 12 small or 6 large
Preparation 15 minutes, chilling 1 hour, assembly 25 minutes, baking 25-30 minutes

You can use bought shortcrust pastry, preferably made with butter, if you don't have time to make your own.

METHOD

1 Break the egg into the water and lightly beat in until combined.

2 Place the flour, butter and salt in the bowl of the processor. Process for 20 seconds adding most of the egg and water. Switch the processor off as soon as the dough forms a ball.

3 Shape the pastry into a round, flatten slightly, wrap in clingfilm and chill in the fridge for an hour.

4 Remove from the fridge 10 minutes before rolling out, to allow to soften slightly.

5 Simmer the peeled and cubed potatoes in a pan of water with a pinch of salt for 8 minutes, then pour them into a colander, quickly place under cold running water to stop the potatoes cooking further, then leave to drain and cool.

6 Heat the oil in the frying pan.

7 Finely chop the onion and crush the garlic, add to the oil, and cook gently but do not allow to colour. When the onions are translucent, take the pan off the heat and allow to cool a little, then add to the potatoes.

8 Grate the cheeses.

9 Place the potatoes and onion mixture in a bowl, add the cheeses, chopped herbs, mustard and cayenne pepper and stir well.

10 Add the cream and combine all the ingredients fully.

11 Add pepper to taste but only a little salt as the cheeses are salty.

12 Set the oven to 200°C fan, 250°C, 475°F, gas 8-9.

13 Grease 2 flat baking sheets and place in the oven to preheat.

14 Lightly roll out the pastry to the thickness of a pound coin (or a dollar or a euro) and cut out 12 rounds. With a wet pastry brush, dampen around the edge of a round of pastry.

15 Place a dessert spoon of cheese mixture down the middle of the round of pastry, lift up two opposite edges and squeeze them together to begin forming the pastie; continue to squeeze along the edges until the cheese mixture is completely enclosed in the pastie. Repeat with all the pastry rounds.

16 To form the wavy edges of each pastie, place your thumb and your index finger on one side of the pastry rim; with the index finger of your other hand, push the pastry between the opposite fingers, continue down the length of each pastie.

17 For the egg wash, separate the egg and place the yolk in a small dish. Add the salt and the water and combine with a pastry brush (the salt helps break down the yolk protein to slacken the mixture), then brush each pastie with the mixture.

18 Take the heated baking sheets out of the oven and place half the pasties on one sheet, leaving a little distance between each one to allow for the pastry to rise.

19 Place the sheet in the oven and repeat the process with the second heated baking sheet.

20 Bake for about 20 minutes; the pastry should be golden and the bases should also be lightly golden and firm.

21 Lift onto a cooling rack, or serve straightaway.

When cool, store in the fridge in an airtight tin for up to five days, or freeze for up to a month.

Herby sausage rolls

Make 12
Preparation 30 minutes, cooking 20-25 minutes

My mum taught me to make rough puff pastry. It was quick and easy and saved so much time compared with making full puff pastry that I continue to use rough puff today.

Don't be put off by the length of the recipe. Once you get up to speed you can make a batch in 30 minutes. But if time is short, bought pastry is fine, and you can always buy sage and onion stuffing too.

INGREDIENTS

For the pastry

400g plain flour plus extra for rolling out (use self-raising gluten-free flour if you prefer)

125g very cold unsalted butter cut into small cubes

125g very cold lard cut into small cubes

2 teaspoons fine sea salt

20ml ice-cold water, you may need a little more or less

1 teaspoon lemon juice

or 500g pack of bought puff pastry.

For the filling

1 small onion, very finely chopped

1 teaspoon of mixed dried herbs

1 teaspoon dried sage

½ level teaspoon fine sea salt

¼ teaspoon finely ground black pepper

500g of good-quality sausage meat, or use vegetarian sausages or 100g of vegetarian sausage-mix

or 50g shop-bought sage and onion stuffing

For the glaze

1 egg yolk

3 teaspoons water

a few grains fine sea salt

These sausage rolls can be served hot or cold. Store in an airtight box in the fridge, or freeze for up to three months.

METHOD

1 Place the chopped onions in a pan, cover with a little water, bring to the boil, and simmer until soft and the liquid is reduced to almost nothing.

2 Add the dried mixed herbs, sage, salt and pepper, stir well to combine, then allow to cool.

3 Alternatively mix the dried herbs, sage, salt and pepper into the bought made-up stuffing.

To make the pastry

4 Place the flour in a large mixing bowl and make a well in the centre.

5 Add the butter and salt. Gently lift the butter and work it into small pieces; do not make so small that it disperses into the flour.

6 Add about three-quarters of the iced water and lemon juice, to make a soft dough. Add a little more water if required. There should still be pieces of butter and lard showing in the dough.

7 Roll into a ball and flatten slightly. Wrap in clingfilm and place in the fridge for 20 minutes.

To continue the filling

8 Place the sausage meat in a bowl and combine with the onion mixture/stuffing. Place in the fridge to rehydrate the dry ingredients a little.

To complete the pastry

9 Flour the work surface, remove the pastry from the fridge and form into a rough rectangle.

10 Roll out to approximately 20 x 40cm, fold into three and give a quarter turn.

11 Roll again into a 20 x 40cm rectangle and fold into three again. Wrap the pastry in clingfilm and chill in the fridge for 30 minutes

12 Repeat the above process twice more, finally wrapping the pastry in clingfilm and chilling in the fridge for 30-60 minutes. You can freeze it at this point, but defrost thoroughly before using.

13 When you're ready to make the sausage rolls, allow the pastry and the sausage-meat mixture to sit on the worktop for 10 minutes to become more manageable.

To assemble

14 Set the oven to 220°C fan, 250°C, 475°F, gas 8 -9.

15 Line and grease 2 baking sheets and place in the oven.

16 For the glaze, mix the egg yolk, the 3 teaspoons of water and salt, and put aside.

17 Lightly flour the work surface and roll out the pastry to a 20 x 40cm rectangle. Cut to create 2 10 x 40cm rectangles.

18 With a pastry brush apply a little water along the long bottom edges of the pastry rectangles.

19 Place half the sausage stuffing into a piping bag with a large nozzle/tip. Pipe a line of stuffing down the centre of each rectangle of pastry, then refill the bag and pipe along the middle of the second piece of pastry.

20 Lift the top edge of the first pastry rectangle, wrap it over the filling, and continue to roll the pastry forward, completely encasing the filling. Turn the pastry over so the edge of the pastry is now on top. With your thumb, press down the edge to seal it; then turn over so it is now on the work surface.

21 Repeat with the second rectangle of pastry, so that you now have two long sausage rolls.

22 Brush off any excess flour from the pastry before brushing the tops only with the egg-yolk mixture. Do not brush right around the rolls as the egg wash will stop the pastry from rising.

23 Using a sawing motion and a serrated knife, cut each long sausage roll into 6 equal pieces.

24 With a pair of scissors, snip 4 equal little incisions in the top of each sausage roll and place the sausage rolls well-spaced onto the hot baking sheets; then place in the oven.

25 Bake for 15 minutes before checking; the pastry should be well risen and golden. Look carefully at the pastry nearest the sausage meat; layers of pastry should be developed and there should be no uncooked pastry. They are likely to take 20-25 minutes to be fully baked.

26 Remove from the oven, place on a cooling rack.

Serves 4-6

Preparation 20 minutes, cooking 1 hour to roast the vegetables, 20-25 minutes to bake the tart

This recipe came about when I had left-over pastry and a few vegetables to hand. You can use ready-made pastry or follow my method in the Herby sausage rolls recipe (page 110). This is the perfect lunch served with salad. You can add any type of cheese: cheddar, feta, ricotta; currently my favourite is goat's cheese.

INGREDIENTS

500g baby tomatoes

1 medium courgette, thinly sliced

3 tablespoons olive oil

a few sprigs of thyme

3 cloves garlic, finely sliced

a few grains of coarse sea salt

a few grains of black pepper

1 quantity of rough puff pastry (see page 110) or 1 pack ready-made puff pastry

3 tablespoons tomato paste

3 tablespoons caramelised onion chutney

1 round of goats cheese, cut in half and then sliced

1 more tablespoon olive oil

1 tablespoon basil, finely chopped

1 more tablespoon thyme, finely chopped

1 more clove garlic, finely chopped

1 egg yolk mixed with 3 teaspoons cold water

a few grains of sea salt

a few basil leaves to decorate

METHOD

1. Preheat the oven to 150°C fan, 160°C, 335°F, gas 3.
2. Place the tomatoes and sliced courgettes on a greased baking sheet and pour over the oil to coat the vegetables. Break up the sprigs of thyme, and sprinkle on with the garlic and seasoning.
3. Place the tray in the oven and roast for 1 hour, turning the ingredients every 20 minutes. Remove from the oven and allow to cool a little.
4. Turn the oven up to 180°C fan, 220°C, 425°F, gas 7.

To assemble the tart

5. Preheat a greased baking tray.
6. Roll the pastry into a rectangle 29cm x 21cm. Use a sharp knife and a ruler to cut the rectangle down to 28cm x20cm.
7. Create a 'picture frame' by placing the ruler along each pastry edge, about 3cm in from the edge, and with a sharp knife, score down into the pastry but not all the way through.
8. Place the tomato paste and the chutney in a bowl and mix until combined.
9. Spread the tomato mixture onto the rectangle of pastry being careful not to go over the edge of the scored lines.
10. Spread the cheese evenly over the tomato.
11. Spread the roasted courgettes evenly over the cheese, and top with the roasted tomatoes. Drizzle the second lot of oil, herbs and garlic over the top of the vegetables.
12. Brush the border with the egg yolk and water glaze, and use a cake lifter to carefully place the tart on the preheated baking tray.
13. Bake for 20 minutes, then check; it should be well risen and golden around the edges, but the middle of the base will probably need a little longer; you don't want a soggy bottom.
14. Remove from the oven after 25 minutes and scatter with torn basil leaves. It is delicious served either warm or cold.

Goat's cheese, tomato & courgette tart

York
Somerton

Special occasions

Puddings are my downfall; given a choice between a 'starter' or a 'pudding', I go for the pud. I once ate two helpings of Huckleberry cheesecake and left out the main course!

Often, I twist the arm of anyone I'm dining with, insisting they choose a different pudding from me so we can share. My reasoning is that tasting puddings is really research and part of my job. It's where I get my inspiration for new bakes and recipe development.

My tip for you is always to ask for two spoons when you order a pudding.

Serves 12

Preparation 15 minutes, cooking 25-30 minutes, decorating 15-20 minutes

Teaming elderflower with sharp tangy lemon curd makes this a winning combination. To make a tiered cake such as the one in the picture, you'll need to triple all the ingredients and use 3 cake tins.

INGREDIENTS

170g eggs, lightly beaten
170g caster sugar
170g soft margarine
170g self-raising flour
4g baking powder
1 tablespoon whole milk
1 teaspoon lemon extract
zest of an unwaxed lemon

Between 3-4 medium eggs but it is best to weigh them out of the shell.

For the cream

1 quantity Chantilly cream (see page 14)

3 tablespoons elderflower cordial or liqueur

1 teaspoon lemon extract

4-8 tablespoons good quality lemon curd (for home-made lemon curd see page 126)

For the lemon drizzle

juice and zest of 2 unwaxed lemons

75g caster sugar

METHOD

1 Set the oven to 160°C fan, 180-190°C, 350-375°F, gas 4-5.

2 Grease and line a 23cm cake tin.

3 Weigh the eggs into a bowl and then add the same weight of sugar, margarine and self-raising flour, plus all the other cake ingredients. Beat for one minute, then allow to rest for one minute before beating for two more minutes (beat by hand or use a mixer). Pour into the prepared cake tin.

4 Bake in the oven for 25 minutes before checking. Cakes love to be listened to – they have so much to say! If they are too noisy then put them back in the oven for another 2 minutes and that should do it.

5 Place on a cooling rack to cool completely.

6 While the cake is baking, prepare the lemon drizzle. Place the lemon and sugar in a pan over a gentle heat, allow the sugar to dissolve and then bring to the boil. Let the pan simmer until the syrup is reduced by a half, then take off the heat and put aside.

To make the Chantilly cream

7 Follow the recipe on page 14.

8 Gradually add the elderflower cordial or liqueur to the Chantilly cream in a steady trickle as you continue to beat on slow until the elderflower is blended in.

9 Finally fold in the lemon extract and 2 tablespoons of lemon curd, and place in the fridge until needed.

To assemble the cake

10 Place a cake board on a cake turntable and use a spoonful of Chantilly cream to anchor one cake layer to the board.

11 Lightly brush the cake layer with the lemon drizzle, then spread with about 3 tablespoons of Chantilly cream. Then gently spread 2 tablespoons of lemon curd on top. Repeat with layers of cake until the last cake layer is added.

12 Place Chantilly cream around the sides of the cake. To create a 'semi-naked' finish take off the excess cream with a cake scraper.

13 Put a size 2 nozzle onto a piping bag and half fill with more Chantilly cream.

14 Holding the bag vertically about 3 cm above the cake, pipe a swirl, and repeat as you like.

15 Put more lemon curd into a separate piping bag, and drizzle over the top of the cake.

Elderflower & lemon celebration cake

Meringues

The fillings can be anything you like.

I weigh mine as it's more accurate than saying '3 egg whites'. I leave them overnight in a bowl covered with a tea towel (so that some of the water from the whites will evaporate).

INGREDIENTS

For the meringue

180g egg whites at room temperature

¼ teaspoon cream of tartar

320g caster sugar

¼ teaspoon vanilla extract

gel food colours, red, orange, yellow, green, blue

For the filling

1 quantity of Chantilly cream, see page 14

500g fruits in season, such as blackberries, raspberries, strawberries, blueberries, mangos, passion fruit

icing sugar to sprinkle on fruit

alternative toppings (optional) such as chocolate chips or mini-chunks

either mint or thyme sprigs to decorate

Makes 12 nests or 8 filled meringues
Preparation 15 minutes, cooking 1½-2 hours

Here's a little tip: to keep your meringues the same size, you can use silicone sheets or baking parchment marked with circles in pencil, to guide the piping (place the parchment upside down on the baking sheet so the pencil won't be in contact with the piped meringue).

METHOD

1. Set the oven to 100°C fan, 100°C, 200°F, gas ¼.
2. Line two baking sheets with either baking parchment or silicone sheets.
3. Place the egg whites with the cream of tartar in a mixing bowl and whisk until the mixture reaches soft-peak stage, then add the vanilla extract and turn the mixer up to high or continue whisking by hand.
4. Gradually add the caster sugar to the egg white, a teaspoon at a time, allowing a few seconds between each spoonful. Continue whipping until the whites are shiny and hold stiff peaks.
5. Take a little mixture between your finger and thumb; it should feel smooth. If it feels gritty, beat the mixture a little more to make sure all the sugar has dissolved.
6. Stand the piping bag, nozzle down, in a large glass. Inside the bag, use a fine paintbrush to paint a line from the bottom up towards the top edge, with your choice of food colours.
7. Place half the meringue mixture in the bag. Don't overfill it, as squeezing it hard would lose some of the precious air bubbles and spoil the texture of the meringue.
8. Holding the piping bag vertically, pipe in a spiral from the centre to the outer edge of one of the marked meringue circles.
9. When you reach this point, pipe on top of the outer circle of meringue; do this three times to build up the sides of the nest, trying not to interrupt the flow of the nozzle. When the nest is the required height quickly pull the nozzle away sideways to finish off neatly. With a wet finger, dab the last piped spot to create a smooth finish.
10. Repeat this with all the meringue circles, refilling the piping bag when required.
11. Bake for 1½-2 hours until the meringues are firm enough to release easily without sticking.
12. Turn the oven off and leave the door ajar to allow the meringues to continue drying out. Two hours is usually enough but you can leave them overnight.

Store in an airtight container until required.

13. To fill the meringue nests, make the Chantilly cream (see page 14).
14. Either spoon or pipe the cream into the nests.
15. Top the cream with the fruits or toppings of your choice and decorate with mint or thyme
16. Just before serving, sift a little icing sugar onto each.

Variation

You can replace the fruit with chocolate chips or mini chunks.

Coffee & pecan Victoria sponge

Serves 8-12, or approximately 24 cupcakes
Preparation 10 minutes, cooking 35-38 minutes, assembly 15 minutes

This cake will store in the fridge for up to three days in a cake box, or you can open-freeze and then place in a container; it will keep for up to a month in the freezer.

INGREDIENTS

For the sponge

All the ingredients should be at room temperature

300g eggs (weighed out of shells – usually 5-6 eggs)

300g caster sugar

300g soft margarine

300g self-raising flour

12g baking powder

1 teaspoon vanilla extract

6 teaspoons instant coffee dissolved in a tablespoon of boiling water, set aside to cool

1 tablespoon whole milk

For the filling/topping

I quantity of buttercream (see page 14)

½ teaspoon vanilla extract

6 teaspoons of instant coffee dissolved in a tablespoon of boiling water and set aside

To decorate

pecans and chocolate-coated coffee beans

METHOD

1 Set the oven to 160°C fan, 180-190°C, 350-375°F, gas 4-5.

2 Grease and line two 23cm cake tins

3 Follow the method for mixing and baking exactly as for Victoria Sponge (page 50), adding the instant coffee at the same time as the vanilla extract.

To fill the cake

4 Make the buttercream icing (see page 14), adding the instant coffee liquid.

5 Place one of the cakes on a cake plate or a board (first place a little buttercream on the base to anchor the cake).

6 Using a spatula, spread half the buttercream onto the cake.

7 Place the second cake on top of the first and press down lightly.

8 Spread half of the remaining buttercream on top.

9 Place the rest of the buttercream in a piping bag fitted with a 2D nozzle, and pipe 12 roses around the edge of the cake.

10 Place a chocolate-covered coffee bean on each piped rose, or a pecan in between each one.

11 Break up about 15-20 pecans and scatter over the cake.

Variation

Put some salted caramel (see page 16) in a piping bag and drizzle a little onto the buttercream filling. Then when you've iced the cake, drizzle a little salted caramel over the top.

Black Forest roulade

Serves 8-10

Preparation for the roulade 15 minutes, cooking 12-14 minutes, for the ganache 10 minutes, chilling 15 minutes, assembly 15 minutes

As a teenager, I thought it was so sophisticated to make a 3-tiered cake sandwiched with fresh cream and cherries, with chocolate grated on top. Nowadays I make a more chocolatey version with more alcohol for family and friends.

INGREDIENTS

For the sponge

5 large free-range eggs at room temperature

140g caster sugar plus extra for sprinkling

60g plain flour

20g cornflour

40g cocoa powder

1 teaspoon vanilla extract

1 teaspoon chocolate extract

For the ganache filling

400g cooking chocolate broken into small pieces (52% cocoa)

20g unsalted butter

560ml double cream

1 tablespoon almond liqueur

150g cherries in syrup (Amarena cherries if possible), plus 1 tablespoon syrup

To decorate

icing sugar to scatter over the finished roulade

edible decorations such as chocolate hearts

METHOD

1. Set the oven to 160°C fan, 180-190°C, 350-375°F, gas 4-5.
2. Prepare a 43cm x 28cm Swiss roll baking tin with baking parchment, greased and lightly floured. Cut baking parchment slightly larger than the baking tin to help when turning out the roulade. Cut a second piece of parchment and place it on the cooling rack.
3. Put the eggs in a bowl and whisk them a little to break up the egg; add the sugar and continue whisking by hand to allow the sugar granules to dissolve. Then whisk the egg mixture on high or by hand for 5 minutes more until light and fluffy. When you lift the beaters, the trail of mixture should stay for a while before slipping back.
4. Sift the flour, cornflour and cocoa powder, a third at a time, into the egg mixture and fold in with a large plastic spatula. Add the vanilla extract after the first third and the chocolate extract after the second third.
5. Pour the mixture gently onto the Swiss roll tin and tilt so it runs into the corners. Don't knock out the precious air bubbles by using a spatula.
6. Bake on the middle shelf, and check after 12 minutes. Do not over-bake; having no fat, the sponge will quickly dry out.
7. When the roulade is cooked, dust caster sugar over the parchment on the cooling rack and turn out the roulade; cool for 2 minutes, then gently peel off the backing parchment, being careful not to break the roulade.
8. Make a shallow cut along one long side (don't cut right through,) this will allow you to begin rolling up the roulade. Roll up steadily and equally with both hands, keeping the paper with the roulade. Then set aside to cool.

To make the ganache

9. Put the chocolate and butter in a bowl.
10. Heat 450ml double cream in a double boiler (or heat-proof bowl over a pan of simmering water), until the cream starts to simmer; pour onto the chocolate and butter, leaving for 3 minutes while the chocolate begins to melt.
11. Whip the mixture with a balloon whisk until light, add the almond liqueur and one tablespoon of syrup from the cherries.
12. Put aside one third of the ganache for decorating the top of the roulade later.
13. Allow the remaining ganache to cool slightly.
14. Whip the remaining double cream and stir gently into the cooled two thirds of ganache.

To assemble

15. Unroll the roulade and spread it evenly with a quantity of the creamy ganache mixture, with slightly less cream at the side where you will begin rolling (first third), then a little thicker (middle third), and finally a little thinner (last third) so that it is easier to roll up.
16. Chop the cherries in half and scatter evenly on the roulade.
17. Roll up the roulade using a fresh piece of parchment paper to help. Don't worry if it cracks a little as the ganache will cover the finished log. With a sharp knife cut off a centimetre from each end of the log to make it tidy (these are your taster pieces!).
18. Spread the remaining ganache over the roulade, using a palate knife to make small brush-stroke movements horizontally across the top and sides of the roulade to make it look like tree bark. Transfer to a serving plate using a cake lifter.
19. Dust the whole log with icing sugar to give a snow effect.
20. At this point you can add chocolate hearts or other edible decorations.
21. Store the roulade in the fridge but remove it an hour before it is to be eaten, to allow the ganache to come to room temperature.

This keeps for two days, or can be open-frozen and then placed in a box in the freezer for two to three weeks. Defrost in the fridge overnight before serving.

Rhubarb, ginger & custard cake

Don't place the sweets on the cake until just before serving as they will begin to dissolve in the cream.

INGREDIENTS

For the rhubarb

250g rhubarb

juice, zest of 1 unwaxed orange

2 tablespoons caster sugar

For the cake

360g eggs

360g caster sugar

140g softened unsalted butter

220g soft margarine

360g self-raising flour

½ teaspoon cinnamon

1 teaspoon ground ginger (around 2g)

6g baking powder

25g custard powder

½ teaspoon vanilla extract

80g preserved ginger cut into small pieces (reserve some of the ginger syrup for the ginger cinnamon cream filling)

For the filling

500ml double cream

1 tablespoon skimmed milk powder

6-8 tablespoons icing sugar

1 tablespoon ginger syrup (from the ginger jar)

¼ teaspoon ground cinnamon

¼ teaspoon ground ginger

¼ teaspoon vanilla extract

To decorate the cake

either some pieces of stem ginger or some rhubarb and custard sweets.

Serves 12-24

To cook the rhubarb 20 minutes, to make the cake 10 minutes, baking 35-40 minutes, assembling and decorating 10 minutes

Caution: the leaves of rhubarb are poisonous and the top part of the stem contains the sap from the leaf. Rhubarb should not be picked after the end of August as the leaf begins to send this poisonous sap down the stems.

METHOD

To cook the rhubarb

1 Set the oven to 150°C fan, 160°C, 335°F, gas 3.

2 Trim top and bottom of the rhubarb, then chop into 2cm lengths and place in a shallow roasting tin, pour over the orange juice and scatter over the sugar.

3 Bake for 15 minutes; it should be soft and beginning to break up; allow to cool a little while you make the cake.

To make the cake

4 Set the oven to 160°C fan, 180-190°C, 350-375°F, gas 4-5.

5 Prepare two 23cm round baking tins, or two square 25cm deep tins, or two 2lb loaf tins.

6 Place the eggs, caster sugar, butter and margarine in a bowl. Beat on low speed or by hand for one minute, then leave for one minute to allow the sugar to dissolve a little.

7 Sift together the flour, cinnamon, ground ginger, baking powder and custard powder.

8 Add the flour mixture to the egg mixture, add the vanilla extract and beat gently, gradually increasing to full speed, then beat for 2 minutes.

9 Fold in the roasted rhubarb and the stem ginger.

10 Pour the mixture equally between the two baking tins, and bake in the oven for 35-40 minutes. If you are using the loaf tins, add Demerara sugar to the tops before baking.

11 The cake is ready when it is golden brown and a skewer comes out clean. Leave in the tins for 5 minutes before turning out onto a cooling rack.

To make the ginger cinnamon cream filling

12 Place the cream in a bowl, whisk in the skimmed milk powder and allow to stand for two minutes.

13 Stir in the icing sugar, ginger syrup, ground cinnamon, ground ginger and vanilla extract and beat on medium or by hand until the cream begins to thicken, occasionally stopping to push the thinner cream on the sides of the bowl into the middle. The filling is ready when it holds its shape.

To assemble the cake

14 Using a serrated knife, cut through each cake horizontally so that you have four layers.

15 Place some cream on the display plate, to help anchor the cake. Place a layer of cake on the plate and spread with 3 tablespoons of the filling; repeat this with two more layers, making sure you have a flat base for the last layer. Spread the final layer of cream evenly on top.

16 Pipe roses on top of the cake, using the rest of the cream in a piping bag with a 2D nozzle. Hold the nozzle vertically 2cm above the cake and begin to pipe from the centre in a round movement to form a rose. Lift the piping nozzle with a twist of your wrist to leave a clean finish.

17 When you have piped 12 roses add a small piece of ginger or a rhubarb and custard sweet/candy to each rose.

Either serve straightaway or place in the fridge to firm up for 2 hours before serving (it can be kept in a fridge for up to three days).

Variation

You can also create a semi-naked cake by spreading cream around the sides of the cake and using a palette knife or a cake shaper to remove the excess.

Courgette, pistachio & lemon cake

INGREDIENTS

For the cake

4 large eggs

250ml groundnut oil

200g caster sugar

zest of two lemons or 8 drops of lemon zest liquid

450g self-raising flour

3g bicarbonate of soda

2g baking powder

2g ground cinnamon

500g of courgettes, grated and placed in a colander over a bowl to drain as much of the water as possible.

200g sultanas soaked in the juice and zest of a lemon with 2 tablespoons of boiling water, so that the fruit plumps up.

75g shelled and chopped pistachios, optional

For the lemon curd

75g unsalted butter

75g caster sugar

125ml freshly squeezed lemon juice

zest of one unwaxed lemon

3 large eggs

For the icing

150g cream cheese

175g sifted icing sugar

juice of one lemon

Makes 12 small pieces or 8 larger pieces or one 20cm cake
Preparation 20 minutes, baking 30-40 minutes, lemon curd 25 minutes

I remember a time when courgettes were simply vegetables you ate with a meal. Then they started to appear in cakes, and I supposed they would be like carrot cake, so why not? I wasn't happy to just follow a recipe but played until I had my perfect bake. I usually make it in summer when I have too many courgettes and my friends bring me their overflow crop too. I do it as a tray bake but it can just as easily be round.

The lemon curd is really quick and easy to make, but you can always use shop-bought. Also, you can buy ready-shelled pistachios, or leave them out altogether. And you can, of course, substitute the lemon with lime.

METHOD

1 Set the oven to 160°C fan, 180-190°C, 350-375°F, gas 4-5.

2 Prepare a tray bake tin 38cm x 28cm (or two 20cm round loose-bottomed cake tins, preferably springform).

3 Place the eggs, oil and sugar in a bowl and beat until light and frothy.

4 Add the lemon zest or lemon extract.

5 Sift the flour, baking powder, bicarbonate of soda and cinnamon into a bowl and then fold into the egg mixture.

6 Fold in the courgettes and then the sultanas, drained.

7 Pour the mixture into the tin(s)and tap down on the worktop to even the mixture out.

8 Place on the middle shelf and bake for 25-30 minutes until a skewer comes out clean.

9 Let it cool in the tin for 10 minutes and then turn out onto a cooling rack.

To make the lemon curd

10 Place the the butter, sugar, zest and lemon juice in a pan and melt over low heat, or use a microwaveable bowl and microwave briefly on medium setting.

11 Whisk the eggs in a bowl, then pour them into the butter mixture, whisking until all combined. Place the mixture in the microwave and heat on medium for one minute, then remove from the oven and whisk, repeating this process until the curd thickens and coats the back of a wooden spoon. If using a hob, place the mixture in a double boiler, and heat for several minutes, stirring regularly until the mixture thickens.

12 Cover with clingfilm and allow to cool.

To assemble the cake

13 With a sharp serrated knife, slice through the tray bake cake horizontally.

14 Spread one half (or one round cake) with lemon curd and place the remaining half (or other round cake) on top.

To make the cream cheese icing

15 Beat the cream cheese until smooth, add icing sugar a spoonful at a time until all combined, then add the juice of the lemon. If the icing is a little slack add a little more icing sugar.

16 Pour the icing on the top of the cake and spread it to the edges, allowing it to slip over onto the sides of the cake a little.

17 Chop the pistachios and scatter them over the top of the cake.

This cake will keep in the fridge for a week but with so much moisture it needs eating within a few days.

Aunty Doreen's gingerbread, raspberry & orange tart (with port wine jelly)

Serves 8-12

Preparation for the port infusion 1 hour, for the base 10 minutes, chilling 40–60 minutes, assembly 10 minutes, 3 hours for the jelly to set; Chantilly cream 10 minutes

My lovely Auntie Doreen introduced me to this delightful easy summer pudding. She was a farmer's wife, up at 6am baking, making and hoovering. She made the tart's base with digestive biscuits; over the years I've replaced these with ginger biscuits. I often make the port infusion in advance.

INGREDIENTS

For the port infusion

pared outer zest of an unwaxed orange

1 cinnamon stick

6 cloves

small piece fresh root ginger, peeled

200ml port

75 ml water

For the jelly

175 ml freshly squeezed orange juice

1 x 5 oz pack raspberry jelly

For the biscuit base

280g ginger biscuits

120g unsalted butter, melted

¼ teaspoon cinnamon

½ teaspoon ground ginger

For the filling

200g fresh raspberries (save 50g for decorating)

For the Chantilly cream

see page 14 and add:

1 teaspoon ginger extract

1 teaspoon ginger syrup (from a jar of ginger in syrup)

METHOD

1. Place the orange zest in a saucepan with the spices, port and water.
2. Gradually heat up to allow the spices to impart their flavours. As soon as it looks near boiling, remove the pan from the heat and leave to infuse for about an hour.
3. Strain out and discard the spices.
4. Heat the infused port to almost-simmering point, then whisk in the cubes of jelly until they're completely dissolved.
5. Strain into a glass measuring jug and make it up to exactly 570 ml with the freshly squeezed orange juice. Set aside to cool.
6. Butter a 23cm loose-bottomed tin.
7. Put the ginger biscuits in a plastic food bag and crush to crumbs using a rolling pin, or blitz in a food processor.
8. Transfer to a bowl, add the melted butter and mix thoroughly until the crumbs are completely coated.
9. Tip into the prepared tin and press firmly down into the base to create an even layer 1-2 cm thick. Chill in the fridge for 40-50 minutes to set firmly.
10. Remove the tin from the fridge. Place the raspberries upright on the biscuit base and gently spoon the cooled jelly over the top. Chill in the fridge at least 3 hours (or overnight, covered with clingfilm).
11. Make the Chantilly cream and set aside in the fridge until needed.
12. To remove the tart from the tin, place the base on top of a tin can, then gradually pull the sides of the tin down. Using a cake slicer, slide the tart onto a serving plate, removing the tin base if you can; if not serve on the base.
13. Swirl cream around the tart, or serve as it is with cream on the side. It is best eaten within a day or two.

This is a good recipe for individual puddings in sundae glasses, using the same layers of biscuit, fruit, jelly and cream.

Index

Acknowledgements

There are so many folk in my life that I need to thank; with their input they made me who I am today.

My Nana Heales, Nanan Croot, Grandma Hetherington, and Grandma Stones all taught me their tips and best bakes; wouldn't they be proud to see their recipes in print (I'm sure they wouldn't mind my tweaks)?

Two mums need thanking: my own Elsie Croot, and Val Stones my mum-in-law; both the original busy bakers, they brought up our families with love and taught me patiently how to bake with love. The smiles on their faces when they presented their bakes will always be with me.

My sisters and brother, Susan, Steven and Denise, have experienced my experimental bakes when I was a teenager and survived to encourage me to write this book. And a really big thank you to Wilhelm, Susan's husband who has always willingly researched things for me on his computer.

Tracy, my sister-in-law, needs a big thank you; without her gentle persuasion and encouragement to apply for Bake Off I would never have got this whole new adventurous life.

To my lovely sister-in-law Annie for her positive support when writing recipes and to Rosie, my niece, for proofreading and attending to my punctuation and grammar as I tentatively began to write.

My sister Denise's husband, Jerry, has been my webmaster and runs my website with care and empathy, he has also sorted out my computer so many time he deserves a medal; thanks Jerry.

Andrew, my nephew, needs a big thank you; he made my first Instagram videos when he was only 14, adding text and music. He inspired me to have a go for myself, showing me how to do things, and the mantra 'you're never too old to learn' could be frequently heard as I battled with new technology. Andrew, I'll never be as good as you but I do try.

Thanks to my long-suffering girlfriends Jen, Bev and Lynne; they were my friends before Bake Off, became my confidantes, acted as food tasters and told fibs as to my whereabouts when I was baking in the tent. They continue to be my tasters for new recipes, and put up with my dottiness.

I especially want to thank JoAnne Cortese, baker, cook, knitter and manager of Pain d'Avignon artisan bread makers in New York. JoAnne and I made friends on Instagram and met up this summer to plan how she could help American bakers access the recipes in my book; she has done an excellent job.

To Harts of Stur and the lovely Clare Smith; your support has been immense, from providing baking equipment to allowing me to write for your magazine.

To the team on the Sherborne Times, Glen Cheyne and Helen Brown, who allowed me to hone my recipe-writing skills for their monthly magazines, as well as giving me permission to use their stock photos of me.

To the so-clever Katharine Davies who took the time to photograph me in her friend Pippa's kitchen and to allow me to use her photos in this book.

Thank you to Vivienne Clore (who taught me that I am worth more than I think I am) for her support in getting this book out on time.

To my Bake Off friends of 2016: Lee, Louise, Michael, Kate, Tom, Rav, Benjamina, Selasi, Andrew, Jane and Candice; I thank you for your love, support and most of all patience while I mess up our WhatsApp chats.

A really big hug for Andrew Smyth and Tom Gilliford who give me their time when I have computer queries.

Thank you Louise Thomas (née Williams), you have been my baking companion and friend for two years; I have learned such a lot from your excellent baking skills.

To my good friends Katie and Glyn from Wots Cooking for having faith in me and for working with me at The British Food Festivals for the last two years. And Howard Middleton, Peter his partner and Sandy Docherty for teaching me how to bake on stage and enjoy a glass or two of wine.

I have to thank Michael Phillips and Jack Ryan-Phillips (Archetype Books) for having the vision that my recipes would make a good book, and thanks too, to Marianne Ryan, for meticulous editing work.

Thank you to all my Instagram and Twitter followers who have been a constant support and encouraged me to write this book; from near and far they have become my extended family; to some I'm Nana Val and to others Aunty Val.

My two grown-up children, Elizabeth and Richarad, deserve a thank you, they have become wonderful loving human beings whom I'm very proud of because they always ate my bakes and never complained when I was busy looking after other folks' children (I calculate 8,000 plus in my teaching career). Now their children, Arthur and William, are subjected to my bakes (and I always hold Henry in my thoughts).

The biggest thank-you must go to my husband, Ian; he promised to look after me 50 years ago and he still does.

I'm sure there are some folk I've missed but you know who you are so thank you too.

Finally if you are reading this, then you bought my book! Thank you, I hope you enjoy baking these recipes with love for your families and friends as much as I have enjoyed baking them.